Smile Across Your Heart

The Process of Building Self Love

Laurie Martin

International Publishers
Saint Paul, Minnesota

Yes International Publishers
1317 Summit Avenue, Saint Paul, MN 55105-2602
651-645-6808

www.yespublishers.com.

Library of Congress Cataloging-in-Publication Data

Martin, Laurie, 1965-
  Smile across your heart : the process of building self love / Laurie Martin.
      p. cm.
  ISBN 978-0-936663-44-9 (pbk. : alk. paper)
1. Self-acceptance. 2. Self-esteem. 3. Conduct of life. I. Title.
  BF575.S37M37 2007
   158.1--dc22
                                                        2007014839

Acknowledgments

I am eternally grateful to the divine and all the beautiful beings in spirit, and to all those here on earth, who assist me in my life.

I'm grateful beyond words for the love my dad and mom gave to me. Thank you so much for allowing me to be who I am, and for all your unconditional love. A special, heartfelt thank you to my brothers, Doug and David, and my sister-in-law, Jodi, and my nieces; you are all very dear to me. Your respect, support, and love brighten my light, and I love you all.

I also want to thank Mary Ann, my closest friend, for her more than twenty years of true friendship, love, and generosity. You're one of the sweetest people I know. Thank you for being such a pillar in my life with all your many caring words, support, and your immeasurable creativity. Speaking of creativity, a very special thanks to my editor, Michael Carr, who is brilliant with the English language.

A heart-full of gratitude to the following friends who have touched my life: Cindy, Ann, Melanie, Carol, Barbie, Carlene, Ricky, Jackie, Sandi, Zach, Shelly, Ashley, Patricia, and Vicki for caring so much about me.

Special thanks to all my workshop attendees, yoga students and teachers, and coaching clients—I'm blessed to be your teacher and to have you as mine!

I send my eternal thanks to my mom, the vice president of my company forever.

Contents

Preface

I hope this book gives you the tools and techniques that will empower you to release your fears and live a more harmonious, courageous, and fulfilled life! My intent is to share the importance of focusing on the humor in life, seeing beauty in yourself and your life experiences, and tapping into a greater awareness of your natural gifts. In short, may you love yourself deeply! I know that you have all the answers inside you, and that my words are the matches that may spark what is already there and what you are meant to hear.

Throughout the book, you will notice that I use the term "the divine" in place of what I refer to as God. Please feel comfortable to substitute any other name or association with the divine that you feel comfortable using according to your life and upbringing.

This book is filled with everyday life-coping skills that most people can relate to. The concepts and principles have proved very effective in workshops and coaching sessions. Eighty percent of what we learn in life is what we experience personally. Therefore, the book is highly interactive—filled with visualizations, prayers, joy journaling, gratitude journaling, affirmations, and requests.

Visualization

Through relaxed visualization and breathing, you can release that busy mind. A one-pointed focus helps eliminate all the mind chatter so we can hear, feel, and see what some call angelic or divine communication coming to us. Getting in touch with your core being allows you to see the beauty of who you are, and the truth of any situation. Quieting the body will quiet the mind. On the physical level, visualization exercises bring health benefits such as relaxation, stress release, decreased anxiety, an enhanced immune system, and lower blood pressure and heart rate.

To prepare for quiet visualization practice, find a space in your home that can serve as your sacred space. It can be in your closet, a corner of your bedroom, or your own special room in your home. If possible, make it a place that is frequented mostly by you, so that it can be kept infused with your own energy. You can create an altar using a table, countertop, or shelf—any place that helps you connect to the divine and your higher self. Special things to put on your altar might include candles, incense, stones or crystals, a book, pictures, or anything that has significant meaning to you. Also place on your altar an intention bowl or jar, in which to hold your intentions and help them manifest.

Intention

Creating an intention is putting in your order to the universe—something like ordering a meal in a restaurant. You are sending out what you intend to occur in your life. You can intend something in any area of your life: the qualities you intend to manifest, what you intend to do, what you intend to have. Believe what you are intending, and trust that it will occur in the right time.

In chapter 3 you will find a detailed description of the process of intending.

Prayer

Prayer is tremendously powerful! This is an opportunity to speak directly to spirit. It's important to send your prayers with love, through the heart. There's no shame in asking for assistance; it isn't as if you were taking the divine or the angels away from something better they could be doing, or someone more deserving they could be helping. Divine beings can assist many people at the same time—I mean, isn't that the whole point of being divine? Release your prayers. Trust that you will be heard; know that if it's for your highest good and the highest good of everyone involved, your prayers will be answered in one way or another, and in divine timing. There is no prayer too big or too small; the divine can assist you—or anyone—with all prayers. Many miracles happen when you allow the divine to help you.

Create your own prayer list. Write down names of people you want to send blessings to. Put this prayer list in your sacred place. You can add to it whenever you want. Imagine a stream of beautiful white light of love saturating and surrounding the list.

Joy Journaling

It's a great idea to have a journal or a pen and pad of paper next to you while reading this book. Writing in a joy journal is a way to focus on all the beauty in your life. Journaling helps you gather up all your feelings, thoughts, wishes, desires, and emotions and put them down on paper.

I have found it most useful to ask the divine and angels questions and then sit quietly for a response while journaling at the same time. When you realize how supported you are in your life, you will feel so much love from the universe that you'll begin to train your mind to look for the joy and the little miracles that occur throughout your day.

Gratitude Writing

Gratitude writing will help you spend a moment of your day to focus on the things you appreciate in your life. Thanking people, situations, and things in your life that have brought you knowledge, love, growth, and happiness will attract more blessings to you. It's important to focus our attention on what we like and appreciate; when we do, we're sending out a higher energy vibration and attracting the same vibration back to us.

Affirmations

Affirmations are phrases used to generate empowering, positive feelings in you and to create your desired reality. Read your affirmations daily or whenever you could use some encouragement. Through them you begin to feel and believe that all things are possible. These positive beliefs begin to attract more positive energy.

Requests

Requests are exercises based on the material in each chapter, which will allow you to experience directly what the text is explaining. I use the request exercises in my life-coaching practice. The requests are assignments that I give to my coaching clients, which are relevant to their life issues or goals that support them to move forward in their desired direction.

Have fun with the exercises, and feel free to modify any of them in whatever ways bring more joy into your life.

Oh, and by the way, to protect the privacy of clients and friends, I have freely changed names throughout the book.

Introduction

My Awakening — A Short but Important Paragraph in My Life

Darkness was strangling me. I was inside a cocoon of fear. I tried to think good thoughts and write down positive affirmations, but the web was just too thick to escape. It had been a full year since I resigned after fifteen years working in corporate America. I had left to pursue my dream of coaching, speaking, teaching yoga, and writing. I was passionate about helping people to love themselves. During that year I had a journey of getting in touch with my own heart. I had put myself under enormous pressure to succeed, to figure out my destiny. I also had big hopes of finding my soul mate. I had a boatload of fear about not knowing my future or how to make it all happen.

As a former corporate vice president of worldwide events, I was accustomed to lots of e-mails and phone calls every day, meetings, complex problems to solve, frequent business trips — feeling that I was needed by, and connected to, many people and projects. After I quit, things got very quiet, and in all that space my self-doubts and fears began bubbling up to the surface. I felt so alone.

Those of you who have gone through a career transition understand the questions: "How am I going to support myself?" "What exactly am I going to be doing?" I didn't trust life enough; I didn't trust myself enough. I thought I was the one in control of my destiny. I put walls of fear around myself. Now, I did save some money before I quit, allowing myself a year to build up my company. But that year flew by, and my savings were drained.

Every morning I would go into my office and try to think of ways to get more business. I checked e-mails frequently; I prayed incessantly. During this time I was successful as a hatha yoga teacher. I taught ten classes a week, and I loved my students. But even with those classes, I didn't get paid enough to support myself. At this time in my life, I was in anguish and pain over a relationship with a man I'll call Bob. Even though I knew that Bob and I were never going to evolve into a serious relationship, I was still having difficulty letting go. It was a casual relationship, no commitments, and it went on and off for over a year. I was searching for love outside myself—giving my power away by waiting for him to call and always being available when he did. It was my deep neediness and loneliness that kept me reaching out to him for a morsel of connection, a little crumb of companionship and love. I felt I couldn't control anything.

I was spiraling downward in a desperate state, with no idea what to do. I seriously didn't know what was happening to me, and I've never been so scared in my life. Feeling as though I was falling apart, I didn't want to be alone anymore. I went to a holistic medical doctor to have blood tests to make sure I was physically healthy. I was. When, with deep sadness, I said to the doctor, "I don't understand what is happening to me," she asked me, "Have you ever heard the term 'nervous breakdown'?" I looked at her and replied, "This is a nervous breakdown?" Not having experienced one before, I found the words terribly serious and frightening. I also went to a "medical intuitive" that I knew and loved. She saw that I was releasing a whole bundle of old behaviors and insecurities. I had no choice but to surrender. She reassured me I was going to be okay; she called it a spiritual awakening.

My father heard the seriousness in my voice when I told him I needed him to fly across country to help me. I remember a moment when my dad was sitting on the couch looking at me; he saw my pain and deep despair. He was sobbing. I knew at that moment that he was scared and this was serious. This was one of the few times in my life I saw my dad cry.

I wrote in my diary: March 19, 2004—My dad just flew in. I'm in a state of anxiety. Thank you, God, for helping me. I allow and accept all divine help from the highest vibration of love. I am done trying to make things happen. I'm done. It's all your time—not my timing. I'm asking myself, what am I afraid of? I'm afraid of not meeting my soul mate; I'm afraid of not sleeping. I'm so tired. I'm just living in the moment. I release all expectations. Please help me, God.

Throughout the next couple of weeks, I was still struggling to teach my yoga classes. Several times, as I entered the gym parking lot, I called my friend Mary Ann from my cell phone. I was telling her, "I don't see the light at the end of the tunnel." I told her I didn't know how I could go in and teach my yoga class. I was tired, and I didn't want to see anyone. My mind was spinning in fear. A few of my phone calls had Mary Ann sobbing and scared for me. Knowing that my dad had already visited me; she called him and shared her feelings about the severity of the situation. From that phone call, which was a week after my dad left, my brother soon came out to visit me.

My Surrender

While my brother was visiting me, my condition continued to worsen. I really didn't even want to leave the house. I wasn't doing much of anything; I wasn't preparing meals for myself and was barely eating, losing weight. I couldn't even watch a television program, because my mind was wrapped in so much fear. I was bone tired! I was in the dark night of the soul. It was the beginning of a deep awakening—my enormous letting go. My brother was leaving my house but didn't want to leave me alone. After about two weeks in this state, I got a phone call from my dad, telling me he had everything worked out. He said he had just gotten off the phone with my lifelong friend Mary Ann, and she wanted me to come and stay with her on the East Coast. I finally had hope! I finally had a plan. I let go and stopped fighting. I booked a flight on the red-eye that night to Westchester, to stay with my best friend and her family. I surrendered.

I canceled a speaking engagement at an upcoming expo; then I gave up all my yoga jobs, left my home and my doctors, and couldn't look back. I had no idea how long I would be gone. I also had to learn to release the beliefs I had about medicine. Just to give you some perspective, whenever I wasn't feeling well, I was accustomed to visiting naturopathic doctors; I ate mostly organic foods and shopped at health food stores. My first inclination over the years has always been to take a "natural" approach.

When I arrived at the Westchester airport in New York the next morning, my friend Mary Ann was the most beautiful sight I had ever seen. I had tears in my eyes. I felt a glimmer of hope. I was invited to stay as long as I wanted, even indefinitely. I felt loved, wanted, and safe. I didn't want to be alone anymore.

Mary Ann was wonderfully nurturing and cooked me one glorious meal after another to fatten me up, so that it didn't take me long to gain back the five pounds I had lost from not eating. Mary Ann and her six-year-old and ten-year-old daughters were fun to be around; we played games, took daily walks, did yoga, rode bikes, and played hide-and-seek, tag, jump rope, and hopscotch. Living so in the moment, I rarely thought about my life in Arizona.

For about a month I couldn't even talk about going back to Arizona. I was focused on healing, being open to receiving, surrendering, trusting, and allowing the healing process to happen along with weekly visits to a very nurturing social worker.

I began to see clearly that it was my perception of my life that had driven me into the frantic state I had found myself in. And in such a state of despair, I wasn't sleeping well, so my mind and body felt exhausted all the time, while my nervous system was in overdrive.

My transformation began through my awareness of my behavior and of the way I perceived my life. And as my vision of myself began changing, I stopped worrying about the future and started to love myself more and appreciate my daily journey. I began to have an inner knowing that I would be okay. I was taking a deep journey into my own heart!

Over a few weeks, as I awakened to deeper levels inside myself, I began to feel better. I began to get enthusiastic about going back home. I was coming to terms with the ending of a relationship, my mother's death, feelings of loss, disappointment, and financial worries. It was an amalgamation of things in all areas that had been building up for several years.

I started making phone calls to pick up a job. After two months in Connecticut, I was on a plane heading home, looking forward to beginning my life over.

Seeing Through New Eyes

This journey was a blessing! I have a deeper connection to everything and myself. I developed a deeper inner peace and trust in the entire earth process and I've never been happier. I live more in the moment. I awakened to my shadow side; I faced my fears. I saw how impatient and disappointed I was with everything in my life. I saw how I was looking for love outside myself, with friendships as well as romantic partners. I gave my power away; I had lousy boundaries. Not comfortable with who I was, I felt a sense of neediness for others' love, approval, and acceptance.

It was a perfect opportunity to look deep within my heart and give myself what I needed. I chose to wake up to the gift, to explore what my heart was calling out for from others, and realized I was responsible for giving myself that love—that I am responsible for fulfilling my own needs. I finally valued myself, trusted my own feelings, and created boundaries by ending relationships that were destined to go nowhere. After seven years living in the desert, I decided it would be nice to be closer to family—within a couple of months of making the decision, I jumped on an airplane and started a new life in Florida.

I now live life more fluidly, enjoying coaching people of all ages and teaching Mastery of Your Heart classes, relaxing visualization techniques, empowerment classes, and yoga.

Nothing can bring you peace but yourself.
—Ralph Waldo Emerson—

Chapter 1
Remembering Your Natural State

You are an eternal spiritual being, and love is your natural state. You may have heard this before, but what does it really mean, in practical terms? It means that you don't need to do anything or be defined by anyone else to prove yourself or to feel validated. The divine made you complete and whole. You need only the true love and acceptance of self. True acceptance means you are worthy of your desires, whatever they may be: a healthy, joyful relationship, a happy, fulfilled career, a serene home life, balanced friendships, a fit and healthy body, and a balanced spirit-and-mind connection. No one can make you feel this way. People can support, encourage, and love you, but you must feel and own that you are created out of pure love and light.

We begin our journey as babies, with light pouring from our spirits through our smiles and sparkling eyes, still connected to purity and innocence. You've probably observed how babies and young children allow their raw emotions and feelings to be expressed. I believe that a major part of why we are here is to remember our divine nature—to own it, to free ourselves of all the pains we hold on to, and know ourselves as holy light beings, connected to the universal consciousness. We are here to evolve spiritually through self-development. We evolve when we understand how important it is to create and do the things we love, to allow our inner song to be sung, and to share our inner magic with the rest of the world in a loving and compassionate manner.

This joy and love is inside every living thing. Have you ever had someone notice that you were tapping your foot or fingers even though there was no music playing? Did you ever catch yourself giggling for no reason? You're expressing your own inner orchestra.

Children seem to find such joy in things that adults take for granted, or maybe just don't see anymore. Why don't we view the world through a child's eyes? Young children have a natural instinct for unselfconscious expression. You can see it in the way they dress themselves, without a care in the world for sophistication and "style." Plaid shirt and striped pants? Orange and red together? You betcha! Or maybe their favorite winter boots with a pair of shorts in summertime. They're proud and enthusiastic about their choices, excited at their mastery and the accomplishment of dressing themselves. They don't care about ideas of what is "correct" in the adult world around them. Why should they? After all, who are we to impose our stodgy old sense of decorum on them if it means stripping them of this pure joy? Why not honor their beautiful self-expression and be proud of them? Yes, even in public! Smile, for this is where the humor is.

I was at my gym one day, at the water cooler, when I noticed two kids, a brother and sister, talking excitedly and looking at something. They were about five and seven, and they exuded such joy and exuberance, I had to see what had captured their interest. I turned around to watch and listen as the little girl exclaimed almost giddily to her brother, "Lookit all these keys!" Her brother responded, "Oh, man, coo-uhl!" Their mother ignored their fascination and simply urged, "Come on, let's go." Glancing over at the keys to see what was so thrilling, I saw that they were all different colors, shapes, and sizes. Somehow, though, I had the feeling that I wasn't quite seeing what the two youngsters had seen, and I wondered why. What filters had I laid over my senses in the years since I was their age?

Children naturally allow their pure joy and wonder to express outward for the whole world to see. I believe, as we grow through our experiences, that we can choose to keep alive our optimism, our curiosity, our wild enthusiasm for life. We can keep seeing the magic all around us and stand in awe before the mystery of it all, still taking time to laugh, play, learn, and love.

This joy is our true nature; it is who we really are. Being silly expresses the heightened state of joy that comes so naturally to kids, and it's important to allow ourselves to be silly, take things a bit more lightly, and keep on believing in miracles. By allowing your enthusiasm to shine forth, you enjoy your life and really feel all your experiences, detached from expectation. Open to spontaneity, and you allow more life to enter your world.

Loving Yourself

Many people spend their lives seeking love and approval from others, never learning that all our needs are truly met by accepting and loving ourselves, by owning that our true nature is pure love. Our self-worth and self-esteem come from inside us, not from parents, teachers, preachers, siblings, friends, or spouse. Without self-love we will continually try to identify ourselves through others and will seek external approval in all areas of our lives. I understand this concept because I was someone who lived this way. It is healthy, wonderful, and important to have support, recognition, love, and connection with others, but at the same time the more we can feel those things inside ourselves first, the more peace we will feel at peace. And we won't feel as though we must have approval from others all the time. Sure, it's nice to get it, but we won't be "aching" for it. It all begins with how you feel about you. If you think you can't live without a particular person in your life, it isn't healthy; it's dependency or code-pendency, which is addictive behavior either way.

As we grow into adulthood, we are responsible for living life according to our own value system, not someone else's. We are born as pure light, and yet, over time, we are the one who dims this light. We darken its luster with thoughts created out of fear and worry, and when we turn away from ourselves, our own light, we are turning away from our connection with the divine. For example, our thoughts of being unworthy or insignificant; not smart enough, rich enough, classy enough, pretty enough, or thin enough; not talented, creative, or intuitive enough, and on and on, endlessly doubting, serve only to keep us fumbling in the dark. These thoughts may pertain to relationships, careers, or our bodies, and may even extend to what's going to happen in the future. One by one, each of these thoughts begins to dim the light. At times these thoughts may be subtle, and we may not realize that our fears are causing them. Observe your thoughts when these fears come in—all those six hundred to two thousand thoughts you have each day that place a shadow over your light. Breathe, and say out loud, "Cancel," and breathe in more positive, self-affirming statements about yourself.

The good news is that we can always lift this veil and begin afresh from a new perspective, a perspective that brings you back to feeling connected to love.

Replace your negative, self-derogating thoughts with ones that are uplifting and life-affirming. You can choose from the following list of affirmations or from the list at the end of each chapter.

- I am worthy of unconditional love, peace, and wealth.
- I am needed here.
- I feel God in my heart.
- I feel the oneness with all there is.
- I embrace and accept all parts of me.

Another way we dim our light is by holding on to the feelings from unhappy memories. It may be just a memory of something someone said to us. In our journey, we make choices of how to perceive our life situations. We also choose what to release. Unless we release the pain and forgive, with every passing year our light becomes a little weaker. The longer you carry around the pains and sorrows of the past, the longer you allow those past feelings and memories to keep your mind in bondage. To allow your light to shine as brightly as possible, begin to notice if there are any areas of your life where you can release and forgive. Notice if you are holding on to unhappy situations too long. Bring yourself back to owning your divine spiritual birthright—your natural state of love. Looking at the fears, make a conscious decision to change the way you believe, accept all of yourself, and notice whether you're giving your power away to someone or something that exists in the present or the past. Know that you are good enough just as you are now.

The very thing we are made of, love, is absolutely free, yet it's worth more than any amount of money can buy. Nothing can break it; nothing can destroy your light. The worst you can do is just temporarily cover it up. With self-love, you are the richest of them all. You will never have to prove anything to anyone, never have to pretend to be anyone else, never have to do anything you don't want to do, and never be held captive. You will be you, in all your ordinariness and all your splendor. The beauty about self-love is that people want to be around someone who is radiating love. Your presence and love alone can heal people. People will gravitate toward you to be in your energy.

Getting to Know Yourself

There are all kinds of benefits to having a close relationship with yourself. A relationship with yourself gives you the comfort of knowing you are enough just as you are—whole and complete, not needing to prove your worthiness or get validation from the world. You will be able to rely on your own instincts, to trust your own guidance and intuition rather than rely on others to direct your life. You will feel more grounded to earth and "inside your body." It is a feeling of comfort and safety to be able to rely on self. This connection with self allows you to accept your beautiful spirit while learning to grow and embrace your insecurities. A strong relationship with yourself keeps you connected to your feelings and your passions—the things that you feel strongly about and that make your heart sing. This brings inner peace.

Once you really know who you are, you will know:
- What you will allow;
- How you want to spend your time;
- How to establish priorities and set goals;
- How to make good decisions;
- Who you want to share your life with, and where you want to live.

Helpful tools for getting to know yourself include quiet time, meditation, visualization, introspection, workshops, faith, prayer, and journaling. Through meditation you relax the mind, gaining clarity, and really see the truth in a particular situation. Visualization creates the energy of your desires, sets it in motion, and helps you focus on where you're headed, on what you want to create in your life. Alone time allows you to go through life taking care of yourself. You will make your own decisions and grow through the experience of learning to be there for yourself.

It's both restful and energizing to spend time each day going within, listening quietly to your own inner voice, and really getting to know who you are through self-observation. This is the only road to true inner peace. Inner peace comes from getting to know who you are on all levels: your personality, your spiritual side, your emotions, your connection to your body and your mind. You'll gain insights into all your fears, joys, desires, hurts, passions, and lessons learned. Quiet time also allows you to have a relationship with the divine. By taking this time, you will have a better understanding of what spirituality is for you. You will hear divine messages. Ask yourself thought-provoking questions. Take time to allow your heart to speak its responses to you. Grab your journal and allow yourself just to begin writing anything that comes to you as a response to these questions: What are you passionate about and why? What are your likes and dislikes? Who is your true self? What are you afraid of? What colors do you feel alive in? What music puts you in a good mood? What is spirituality to you? What song do you sing the most? What are your favorite foods? What art do you enjoy? What are your favorite flowers to smell and to look at? If you could have any car you want, what car would you drive? Why? What kinds of movies do you like to watch? What kinds of charities are you drawn to? Do you like to live near water? Desert? Mountains? Woods? Some other environment? What is your favorite herb? What do you like to talk about? What are your thoughts on life after death? What home styles do you like? Modern? Traditional? New? Older? Are you a cold-weather or warm-weather person? What books and magazines do you like to read? What are your values? How do you want to live your life? What do you want your kids to say about you? If you had five million dollars, how would you spend your time and money?

It's vitally important to get to know ourselves intimately, to the core of our beings. To some this may be scary, but when we find that place, we find our authentic power.

Doing the things we're passionate about opens the doorway to true fulfillment and success. The more we do the things we love, the more our inner light shines, and the more light we draw to ourselves. Just look at pictures of yourself in your photo album. You can see light emanating from your eyes when you are doing things you enjoy, or when it was a happy time in your life.

Become your own observer, and at times you may find that you're downright humorous. You will find yourself laughing at yourself and even at your own insecurities. Be aware of your insecurities when they come up. They are not you; your divine nature isn't insecure. Observe yourself as others trigger your insecurities. Notice how you feel; allow yourself time to check in with yourself, to uncover what is really going on. What is making you uncomfortable? It may take a little while to get to the root of it, but the better you get to know yourself, the more in tune you'll be with your feelings, and the quicker you will identify your insecurities and strengths. When things seem overwhelming, take one step at a time; don't jump ahead. Always take a deep belly breath when you catch yourself thinking in an unproductive or unhelpful way. Ask if you are personalizing a situation. Pray and ask the divine to help you feel more empowered in that particular area of your life.

Many people feel insecure in anticipation of attending a big party or gathering where they don't know anyone. The comfort in this is, most people feel that way, too. And if you take the focus off yourself and put it on finding interesting things about the people you're going to meet, it will help you to relax and feel more comfortable. Honor your insecurities. If you know you don't like big parties full of people you don't know, don't make yourself feel as though something is wrong with you. Not many people enjoy going to a party where they don't know anyone. Don't feel bad; do what you feel comfortable doing. You can try imagining the situation as a positive one and see if that changes the energy for you. The insecurity may be from a memory of a past occurrence, projecting onto the future event.

Observe whether you are one of those people who live with a lot of external noise and stimulation in your life. Do you wake up in the morning and put the radio or television on, get in your car and put the music on and get on the cell phone, and have music playing when you're at work Every few days, experiment with driving or working without any radio, telephone, or television to distract you from listening to your own inner voice, or take one day a month in solitude.

Journaling is a great way to listen to your inner voice, to observe your feelings and thoughts. It's also a great way to allow stuff to come up and then release it onto the paper. You can write to the divine; let God know how you feel and what you're thinking about. Ask the divine questions and listen to what you hear or just let the pen do the writing. A half-hour evening hot bath with Epsom salts, apple cider vinegar, essential oils, candles, and burning sage, eyes closed and nothing to do but breathe, is another great way to let go and go within, pray, or meditate. Have patience with yourself, and be gentle and nurturing.

Take short breaks during your busy day, and tune in to how you feel. The first step is introspection, an essential part of figuring out who we are. This can be difficult for people who were not raised in a family where they felt safe to express their emotions and feelings. Our emotions are the "action" that occurs from our thoughts and feelings. Once we acknowledge our emotions, we can then choose what to do with them, how to express them, and how long to hold on to them. Once the emotions are in play, our thought forms can either amplify or diminish them. Our emotions create real physiological effects in the body. For example, if you're anxious about giving a speech in front of a live audience, you can give yourself a stomachache. Or if someone who is nonconfrontational experiences a great deal of fighting around him at work, he can become so stressed and nervous that by the end of the day, he leaves work with a headache.

We choose how much power we give to our emotions, and we can decide how to perceive a particular emotion. If we don't judge the feeling as negative and we see it as just an emotion, we can separate ourselves from the experience and not label it. Identify the emotion. We can say, "I'm having an experience of nervousness right now, and this, too, shall pass." Take a few slow, deep breaths. Become a third-party observer, and remember, all emotions change; they don't stay forever.

Many people dull their senses and feelings by burying themselves in work or using drugs and alcohol, without ever taking the time to be quiet. They blame their job, the location of where they live, the type of people they are "forced" to associate with, and all manner of outside situations. But the work must be done on the inside so then you will attract what you really believe you are ready for and deserve. By trusting the divine and ourselves, dismantling the walls of fear, we are allowing space for miracles to happen. We have specific experiences in our lives in order to learn about who we are, to trust ourselves more, to love ourselves more. Think about the experiences in your life that have given you those opportunities.

The Path to Becoming Your Own Best Friend

Think about your loyalty and love in your relationships with your family. What are the feelings of unconditional love that emanate from you toward that person? Give the same feelings of unconditional love and respect to yourself. Each day, look into your own eyes in the mirror and say, "I love you, _____, because _____ _____." (Insert your own name and say why you love yourself in that moment.)

Being your own best friend means you can really rely on yourself to be the President of You, which includes all the things on the following page. As you read this self-love list, take inventory of the things you already do.

Rest when your body is tired; express your authentic feelings and opinions by speaking up for yourself; take care of daily hygiene; keep your environment clean and orderly; eat healthy foods; hire professional help when you need it; go to appropriate doctors for annual checkups; say no to a date or social situation that doesn't feel right for you; buy yourself nice things; get out of unhealthy romantic relationships, jobs, and friendships; live balanced in body, spirit, and mind; pay bills on time; help others in need; establish healthy boundaries; do the things you enjoy; attend uplifting events; seek out opportunities; question authority; feel a sense of freedom of expression; make responsible choices that reflect your values; move forward toward your goals and dreams with perseverance; be honest with yourself and others; allow reflective time to unwind; express gratitude, and forgive; be accountable for your commitments; speak kindly to yourself; allow your playful side to come out and have fun; have patience and tolerance for yourself.

You are creating true self-reliance; you are showing up for you and taking care of yourself! You are making choices that honor your heart. Are your expectations very high? Notice if you fail to live up to an ideal or expectation you have placed on yourself. Know that you are doing the best you can in all your endeavors, and respect and honor that. Have patience and tolerance with yourself. This is the path to becoming your own best friend. You respect and accept your friends just as they are without trying to change them; this is true friendship, true unconditional love. Give yourself this same love and respect. Be at peace with who you are.

Sometimes we can take our own growth for granted and don't recognize our accomplishments. Try to acknowledge your accomplishments daily to yourself—the things you are proud of. Write them in your journal: For example, My Action taken: I expressed how I felt to my doctor today, and I feel much better; we had a nice conversation. Accomplishment: I am a really good communicator.

I'm proud of myself for my communication skills and for having the courage to speak up.

Examples of accomplishments:
- You had an insight or solution, a creative new idea.
- You went somewhere by yourself: movies, restaurant, vacation.
- You allowed yourself to be vulnerable.
- You expressed yourself to someone to clear the air.
- You admitted a mistake.
- You chose not to take a comment personally.
- You chose not to make someone else wrong.
- You forgave yourself or someone else.
- You looked for the positive in a situation.
- You took action toward your goals.
- You helped someone feel good about himself or herself.
- You saw the beauty in someone you normally haven't liked.
- You sent blessings to people.
- You had a strong sense of trust in the divine.
- You stayed open to hearing someone else's point of view.
- You were proud of your decisions and choices.
- You were proud of your focus and determination.
- You had the courage to tell the truth.

People often say to me, "Wow, I can't believe you cook a whole meal for yourself for dinner; if it were just me, I'd nuke a frozen dinner." If you enjoy nice meals and cooking, try making nice meals for yourself. Why do we have to make nice meals only for our family or guests? Why not treat yourself like a friend as well as a guest? Make yourself a healthy, mouthwatering meal, and have a special dinner with yourself. Yum! The point is, live your life now and treat yourself like the most important person in your world. Don't stop your life in any way, waiting for a future event. Do the things you want, and if that means going out and buying a house, traveling, getting a pet, getting in shape, do it! Live fully today.

Do things that nurture and respect your spirit. Have the courage to be alone and not care what others think. Know how wonderful you are without anyone's approval. Being your own best friend means you can enjoy going out by yourself without feeling uncomfortable. You can go on vacation alone and do all the things you want to do. If there's a movie you want to see, you don't have to wait for someone to go with. Just go and enjoy the movies, and buy yourself something to eat, too! Enjoy going to your favorite restaurants. (One thing we know for sure, you'll enjoy the conversation!) Take hot bubble baths, rest, read, attend workshops, get a massage, listen to your favorite music, sing, play, and laugh.

The Beauty of Observing Your Patterns

If you hit the rewind button on your life, you may see particular patterns that occurred to teach you something. Once we identify the pattern, we can look inside and take inventory of the insecurities that have caused us to repeat similar relationships or situations. These repeating patterns are lessons for us to learn and grow from. Until we understand our part within these patterns, we may continue to create the same patterns for many years. The big moment of truth comes when we recognize how our energy attracted those experiences. We see firsthand how this pattern is mirroring back what is going on inside us. The great news is, now we can change and stop those patterns. We can give ourselves what we are looking for from others or from outside situations. We end the cycle, and we will never be the same person again. We change our perceptions and beliefs, and in return our energy will not attract the same vibration into our lives.

For example, let's say your friend Alexa is bossy and controlling. Alexa has always chosen when you would socialize together and where you would go. The relationship has pretty much been dictated by her, and you have allowed this. One day you feel sad and hurt because she is only available on her terms and isn't there for you when you need her. You decide to stay in the friendship, even though you are still hurt.

Alexa has given you a gift: the opportunities to set up boundaries for yourself, own your own personal power, and express yourself. You will understand that you are worthy and deserving of a more balanced friendship.

Now, let's say you chose not to do any of these steps fully. Don't worry; the universe will supply you with other opportunities to learn these lessons. Indeed, you may have already had similar relationships. You will have another friendship or romantic relationship in which similar issues will arise.

This will now be a pattern until you fully embrace the lessons and say, "Okay, I get it. I choose me. I've been giving my power away, making myself available, and generally being a doormat for Alexa. I'm worthy enough for a friend to be there for me and do things I want to do, too. I'm going to talk to her and inform her of my expectations, tell her what would honor me. If she's okay with that, then we can continue our friendship. If not, this relationship will change." Then bless her regardless of how she responds.

We are here with our own specific scripted core lessons to learn in this lifetime, and learning them helps to guide us back to our true selves. Alexa is a gift for you. She is highlighting your insecurity, or a belief, giving you a gift by showing you what you are missing inside.

Identifying our patterns in life will help us uncover the key to learning our lessons. It's about taking responsibility for our actions, thoughts, and feelings. What were you expecting to get from those people, places, or jobs?

- Any patterns with repeat types of arguments?
- What are the commonalities with each person?
- Any repeat patterns in the types of friendships or people you are attracting?
- What have you learned in your family relationships?
- What have been the repeat patterns in your jobs?

Give yourself what you were looking for from others. Love and value yourself more than anyone else. Know that you are worthy of healthy relationships and a healthy work environment. Other people come into our lives to mirror back to us our own insecurities; we are learning and growing in these relationships. If we go through life blaming everyone else or thinking everyone else is acting or behaving inappropriately, then we aren't learning. If we take responsibility and stop blaming the other person or situation, we can see what the bigger picture is showing us: our insecurities. This is an opportunity to say, "I get it! I attracted this person into my life to show me how needy I am. This person was mirroring what was going on inside me."

Where are you not meeting your own expectations? Write it out in your journal. If we ache for love or yearn for approval from another, we assume we lack this love inside. We assume we need something outside ourselves to make us complete and happy. We can switch our focus to choosing to give ourselves what we perceive is lacking. You don't lack anything. You are a spirit connected to the divine.

Try the following exercise:

1. Go into the feeling of what you perceive to be missing. What is the thing you feel you are lacking? Ask, "What is it that I want?"

2. Notice whether you are looking to another person to provide what you think is missing from your life.

3. Release the yearning to the universe. Invite the divine into your heart and ask for help to feel your own love. Ask for healing to

occur in any area that you perceive to be lacking. Ask the divine for a new beginning, for a new power of self-love and full acceptance of all parts of who you are now—for a new, healthier vision of yourself so that you no longer live inside this fear. Ask the divine to bring light to the areas of darkness and to open your heart to more love by helping you let go of those feelings and emotions that don't serve you. Start focusing on the feelings of what you do want in your life. Say to yourself, "I'm connecting with the universal consciousness and attracting to me the highest vibration of love, peace, joy, wealth, healing, happiness, and abundance.

4. Take a deep breath; hold the intention of breathing in that vibration. Fill yourself up with all the feelings and emotions of love and approval.

5. Do you remember how special and happy you've felt on your birthday or some other special day? Go back to those feelings and bring them into your whole being. Feel them penetrating into your bloodstream, your cells, muscles, ligaments, bones, organs, brain, skin, soul, and spirit. Feel love with all your senses: What is the temperature of this love? What is its color? What does it smell like? Does it have a texture? See your body light up and glow with your own magical love! See and feel it go deep inside the shadows inside you. Keep looking at yourself with those adoring eyes! Keep expanding your limitless vision of yourself. See yourself already living in a manner and lifestyle that you desire.

Be thankful to all the teachers in your life who mirror back to you your insecurities. They have all assisted in your growth. I believe we made agreements with these people, before we came here from the spirit world, to learn these lessons and grow wiser. The anger you might feel in reaction to what others say is really anger or sadness you feel toward yourself or your life. Remarks from others may hit a sore spot within you that you haven't yet come to peace with.

When you see the pattern, growth occurs. You passed. Hurrah! Allow and acknowledge your humanness, and trust that you're doing the best you can. Appreciate exactly where you are today.

Changing, Growing, and Evolving

As we are living life and growing, our life experiences build upon one another. There are many, many layers of building blocks leading to full acceptance and God-realization. Each block of growth represents an increase in our conscious awareness. They are blocks of love, joy, trust, faith, and compassion. Each layer we grow into will bring us closer to our true nature, a higher vibration, allowing a deep connection with our life purpose and our heart. We do this by understanding more about ourselves; you can call it self-mastery. Have you ever read a spiritual or self-help book, watched a spiritual movie like *What the Bleep Do We know!?* or listened to an inspirational lecture again and again and found the material to be richer several years later? It's because you are richer. You have more depth, and the capacity to take the information into your awareness in much deeper levels of comprehension.

As this example unfolds, you will see how a woman graduated to another level of compassion. Jill was judgmental toward certain people, with an especially low tolerance for people who didn't listen and follow directions. Jill considered them slow, with low self-esteem. Each time she spotted people in this category, she would have those thoughts about them. One day Jill was thrown into a new role, with an entirely unfamiliar task and a new group of people. She didn't know what she was supposed to do. Along with feeling stupid, she also felt the disapproving feelings from the woman she was working for. Jill was upset by the energy she was getting from this woman, which increased her own negative thinking, so that she felt her self-esteem spiraling downward.

The woman's energy and thoughts did not help Jill. But Jill had an epiphany; she saw how her judgments of others came back to her. She learned to have more compassion and patience for others who are learning to do new things. Jill felt what it was like, and realized that every time she judged others it was only adding to their own insecurities. And she grew from this experience. She had identified her own behavior and felt firsthand how her thoughts toward others may have made them feel. She grew into another level of compassion.

We learn as we go through life and gather experience through taking risks, trying new things, one step at a time; and like puzzle pieces, these experiences build on one another. We learn by being aware of what we are thinking and feeling, and taking responsibility. Our external world matches our inner world, acting as a magnifying mirror, highlighting what we have inside ourselves.

Let's say you have a vision of being a successful artist; you will undergo growth within yourself in increments. The first increment may be to feel that you are a good enough artist to paint; the second, to say openly that you are an artist; and the third, to give yourself the proper time and space to paint without feeling guilty about doing something that isn't bringing in money, as would, say, a nine-to-five job. Then you may have lessons of growth in feeling confident enough to promote and sell your work to galleries. Your own confidence is building as you are blooming into an accomplished artist. Over time, you will be able to hear criticism and feedback without taking it personally, and then you may continue to gain more confidence and perhaps teach art or take your work to another level, depending on your vision.

When we're doing something new, we have a different feeling from when we are "seasoned." Our patience, faith, and determination will be tested, and our inner strength will keep us going. As we continue toward our dreams, one day at a time, the universe supports us. Every step in our lives is needed to create the whole path. We can't jump to the end of the path without taking all the steps in their proper places. So enjoy the path—one step at a time.

The universe gives to us what we are comfortable with at that particular time and place. If you think you're ready for more than you currently have in a particular area of your life, you need only look within yourself and see if there is any insecurity, fear, or a feeling of not being good enough that could be holding you back. By observing what we're thinking about, we can notice if these thoughts are hindering our forward motion. Or an energy block may be what's holding us back. An energy block is a construct of thoughts or beliefs from a previous situation that is still in our energy field and needs to be cleared and released. I have found this a helpful prayer to use: "Please release from my energy field any blocks formed of unhealthy emotions, beliefs, and thoughts from my past or from other people that are keeping me from achieving my desires. Please fill my energy field with divine love."

As we change, grow and learn, we are evolving and don't energetically attract the same experiences into our lives. When we change and really learn those lessons, life around us changes. Each cycle gives way to create a new phase. We may not be attracted to the same people for romances or friendships. As our self-esteem has increased, so has our vibration, because we are filled with more love and compassion. An increase in love is a higher vibration. We attract a higher vibration of people, opportunities, and experiences into our lives, and on a deeper level of intimacy. As we grow, our perceptions, views, attitudes, and desires change.

If you were single today, would you date the same people you dated when you were in high school or college? Maybe you married that person; if you met him or her today, would you still marry them? They may have grown along with you in a healthy way, too. How you feel about yourself is a direct reflection of how you respond to the world, to life, to situations. How much your heart is open to yourself is how much you are open to others. Much of the time we may not even be aware of our growth. Growth is achieved when you are not responding or reacting in the same way you used to.

People are in your life to help you grow. If we didn't have relationships with people, we wouldn't have all these opportunities to learn patience, love, compassion, tolerance, and forgiveness.

Trust Yourself

Trust in the love you are made of. You are a part of the divine, created from the divine. How could you not be worthy? Trust in the divine and in your connection with everything. Trust in the importance of your part in the whole universe. Know that there is no separation between you and spirit and there never can be, for you are spirit. You're just renting your body in this lifetime; your body is not who you are. In order to trust yourself, you must really be able to rely on yourself. Trusting yourself means you live life by

- Being consciously present;
- Living responsibly;
- Following your inner guidance;
- Having courage and faith;
- Making good choices.

Living consciously means you are showing up for your life wide awake to the good, the difficult, the unhappy and happy moments. You are not avoiding, blaming, making excuses, or running from uncomfortable feelings or situations. You have the ability to handle anything that comes your way. You are observing your actions, feelings, insecurities, and reactions—hopefully with some humor.

Part of trusting life is having faith that everything is always in divine order. In the midst of big life changes, we have an understanding that there is a divine order, whether we see it or not. Friendships may change or end in our lives as we grow and expand, but this is healthy and a part of the life process. It may not feel so good at the time. When things happen that cause us discomfort, in time we can get into that higher understanding that this may be for our best and highest good. Maybe new opportunities or new people will enter our lives. We trust that new friends will come along. We try not to take it personally when this happens. We bless our friends, learn something from each friendship, and stay open to new friendships. This may be some kind of a lesson in letting go, faith, staying positive, and seeing the glass as half-filled. This creates room for new experiences. Maybe we were done learning from one another at that time and, without any discord, it was the natural time to go our separate ways. During change, see if you can stay in a space of trusting that good things will flow into your life. During sad times it can be challenging, but trust that there's always a reason for everything that occurs.

Remember, the light is always there, and you will soon see it! If you trust yourself to be there for "you" when things don't go as you expect, you will be able to have a positive attitude. Try to imagine the best possible scenario. For example, if you get replaced in a job, you know that your time was meant to be spent somewhere else. Try to have the mind-set and "heart-set" that your energy will attract a better job for you or that the universe needs you somewhere else.

Good decisions are choices that honor our spirit and our heart. Good choices are for our highest and best good. These choices usually benefit others as well. When making these decisions, notice how your body feels. Scan your body and see if you feel comfortable or uncomfortable. Spend time contemplating or meditating before making big decisions. Pray for help, for clarity and clear guidance for your highest good. Notice what shows up in your life to support or not support your decision. Imagine the end result after choosing each of your options. Which option makes you feel better?

A friend of mine was put in a precarious situation with a family member when the family member asked him to provide a service at a discount. My friend felt a strong sense of family obligation to do it, but on the other hand, he really didn't want to. I asked him to imagine what he would feel like if he provided the service at a discounted rate. How would he feel afterward? I also asked him to imagine how he would feel after he politely said no. He followed through on my suggestion and made a decision based on honoring himself. He said no and was very pleased with his decision in the end.

The more we make decisions that we are proud of—that honor our values—the more we will feel that we can depend and rely on ourselves. These experiences build on one another. We then feel that we are dependable and self-reliant. If honesty, for example, is one of your key values and you're in a relationship with a partner and you made the choice to have an affair, you will not be making a decision that honors your heart or respects what you believe in. When making decisions, ask yourself, "Does this bring me closer or further away from my desired goals? Does it honor my values?"

When you are unsure about a particular situation or concerned about something, ask yourself these questions and write your responses in your journal:

- What does your heart say?
- What can you do to move forward in your desired direction?
- What does your higher self say?
- What does your perfect scenario look like?
- What are you already doing to support that?

A big part of trusting ourselves is feeling connected to our own guidance, or intuition. A familiar term most people know is "gut feeling." Begin paying attention to how you feel about things, and act according to how you feel. If you are receiving messages, guidance, or a gut feeling about a person, pay attention to this information and find out whether it's accurate. You can do the same thing when you're in conversation with people by guessing, before they finish their sentences, what they were going to say.

Notice if you

- Think of someone out of the blue and then they call you or you see them that day or the next.
- Guess who's calling on the phone while it's still ringing.
- Sense what's troubling someone deep inside while they are speaking to you about something else.
- Receive insight while you're in the shower, driving, swimming, running, walking, out in nature.
- Receive a different message from what someone is telling you.
- Get goose bumps or chills when you or someone else is speaking about something.
- Sense if someone has positive or negative energy.
- Receive the same information from multiple sources in a short time span.
- Get vivid pictures or images of something.
- Have insightful, detailed dreams.
- Smell strong scents.
- Hear or see spirit talking to you.
- Receive a piece of wisdom or insight and then notice that others are writing about the same information.

Spirit guides us to specific information in magazines, on the web, television, radio, through movies, books, and other people, to help us with things we may have been thinking about or questioning. Keep track of this information. The more you listen to your guidance, act on it, and then figure out if it's correct, the more you will trust yourself. The more you do this, the less you will second-guess or doubt yourself. Everyone has the ability to be intuitive; trust yourself and trust what you're sensing or feeling. Be especially attentive if you hear the same message or information two or three times. Most likely, you have had your own special experiences with divine messages or sensing the spirit of a loved one around you.

Guidance and intuitive information come to us in various ways: telepathically (through the mind), empathically (through the senses, feelings, and emotions), clairvoyantly (seeing images, pictures, places, spirits, and objects beyond our normal senses, through the "third eye," or mind's eye). Clairsentience senses spirit, feels physical sensations, or gives an inexplicable "knowing" about something or someone. Clairaudience hears information from spirit, whereas clairolfaction is the ability to smell spirit, illness, or other things through a nonordinary ability. Notice how you receive your information. If you are interested, there are several good books on the subject. I recommend *Intuitive Wellness* by Laura Alden Kamm; also, Laura Day has a wonderful book called *Practical Intuition.* Through meditation, practice trusting your own intuition. Ask your guidance for help.

As I was beginning to trust my own guidance more, I realized it wasn't necessary to get others' opinions on certain things in my life. I began keeping information closer to my heart, holding on to the sacred energy that only I was creating around ideas, dreams, projects, or feelings. I was then more confident in the decisions I was making. Living in such a way, we are ensuring that our desires are being supported with the same positive vibration. Others aren't connected to our heart in the same way we are; they may not see or feel the same passions. Everyone has their own life path, specific life lessons, and his or her own experiences and ways of understanding life. Others' opinions, no matter how well intended, aren't necessarily for our highest good. It's imperative to trust our own guidance. Once our idea has become tangible or has taken form, we can share with others, but when we're excited about a vision or dream, it's prudent to hold the sacred energy close to the heart. Have you ever been so excited about a very precious idea that you shared it with someone, only to find that after you shared it, the energy diminished because your friend didn't respond as excitedly as you had hoped? Keep the energy sacred; keep it to yourself for a while.

What is the most courageous thing you've ever done in your life? What did you learn from it? Courage gives you the ability to leave unhealthy relationships, friendships, environments, or careers. It allows you to ask for a raise when you deserve one, ask for a job transfer or strike out on your own when you want to relocate, or speak to your partner or a family member about something that is upsetting you. Courage means that you believe you have choices and can begin a new life at any moment; that you believe there is a way out of every unhealthy situation, that you believe in your dreams and that you move toward your dreams by taking action.

Building Confidence: Expanding Knowledge and Taking Chances

I believe that throughout life our self-esteem changes, and can change day to day, depending on what is going on in our lives. We all have areas where we are more confident than in others. One way we learn to feel good about ourselves is by expanding our knowledge in particular areas of interest. It can be a vulnerable feeling when we begin things that are new or foreign to us, but that's where the growth occurs. This is an opportunity to face insecurities that may arise: fear of failure, fear that you're not going to be liked, fear of saying something silly, of being judged, of not having anything valuable to say or not having all the answers. When you do things that are challenging you to move out of your comfort zone, allow your insecurities to come to the surface, and move through it, you create opportunities for learning and building confidence. You gain new perspectives and go beyond your perceived limitations.

Participate in activities that you enjoy. Your heart will rejoice as you dive into a deeper exploration of your creativity. Learn a new skill; make a new discovery; find a new passion, sport, or hobby. Take a pottery or writing class, join a hiking club, take singing lessons, learn to play a musical instrument, learn about another religion, sign up for a cooking class or dance lessons, start a sewing project, read the classics, create a scrapbook, volunteer your time to a child, build a piece of furniture, take a painting class, learn about finance and investments, plant a garden, take a computer class, decorate your home, attend a workshop, move to a new place, take tennis or sailing lessons, begin a new relationship. Get certified in something that represents a real passion for you. Expand your horizons spiritually and creatively.

When we listen to our intuition and do the things we're truly interested in, we improve our self-image, feel a sense of achievement, and grow wiser. Wisdom comes from an accumulation of learning experiences: life lessons, conscious awareness of the energy you are sending out and how it is drawing situations to you, and responsibility for your life outcomes. When you live life awakened, you can learn through harnessing your wisdom. We don't have to learn through pain.

Our sense of achievement is determined in part by the way others respond to what we are doing or creating. The direct feedback that our actions generate acts as a compass, guiding us in a particular direction. As we get more confident at something, we know and feel that we are truly doing the best in any situation, and it doesn't matter so much what others think. We don't even question ourselves or need feedback from others. What areas of your life are you confident in?

We are all confident in various areas of our lives. You will notice that the more confidant you are in a particular sphere, the more easily that area seems to flow in your life. If you're confident in romantic relationships, you may have had it easy most of your life in that sphere. If you're athletically inclined, your body probably adapts well to new physical activities. If you are intellectually gifted, you may have done well in school and feel pretty confident in academic pursuits. Whatever your particular set of skills, your endeavors in those arenas are more likely to flow smoothly.

Now take a look at the areas you are not so confident in. Pick one, and increase your skill and knowledge in it. You will be giving yourself the opportunity to grow. Don't get discouraged if life doesn't always go your way. The most successful people have met the greatest challenges. Abraham Lincoln is a good example. A couple of his businesses failed, he lost several elections, his fiancée died, and a year later he had a nervous breakdown; but finally, at age fifty-one, he became the president of the United States. Most millionaires have had big losses in their lives, but they have had the drive and conviction to try again and again. So don't give up; keep on going, one day at a time.

Continue doing the things you love. We gain confidence when we take chances and make good choices. We build our confidence by being able to rely on ourselves. Ask the divine to help you have the courage to follow your heart. Ask the divine to show you new avenues for doing the things you love.

Chapter 2
Staying True to Yourself

We use our personal power all the time, in all kinds of circumstances. Personal power comes from having a sense of control over your own life, a sense that you believe you have the power to make choices, and allow your own love to flow. It comes from believing that you can achieve what you want, that you can take chances and go after your dreams. We use our power to speak our truth, to express who we are in the world, and to handle everyday life and business by honoring our needs. And on the flip side, we can also give our power away. When we are not in our power and our self-love, it means we

- Fear losing someone or something;
- Fear hurting others;
- Give our power away to others or to old memories
- Put people on a pedestal;
- Think we are not worthy of something.

Whenever we are not in our power, we aren't listening to our inner voice or our body, not paying attention to what we want. We get that feeling of losing ourselves and not trusting, of playing small and being afraid to say no, of not recognizing our own worth. And in this state, we can make compromises. Over time, compromising our needs and our desires can create resentment, and not communicating how we feel can eventually hurt our spirit.

Many women have shared with me that they too easily give their power away to men, careers, kids, in-laws, friends, parents, or someone else. They feel that they have lost themselves in the day-to-day activities of raising a family, and their energy is constantly going out to meet others' needs before their own. Naturally, there will be times when others have more knowledge or expertise in a particular area, but that doesn't make us "less than" or inadequate in any way. It just makes us open for learning. If you know something, express it. No one benefits when we play small.

Take a look at the areas in your life where you feel controlled or unempowered in some way. If you feel that a job or a person has control over you, it's a great opportunity to discover why you feel powerless in that area, and to take your power back. Ask yourself if you feel any of the above bullet points. Decide to love yourself more than what you fear.

In going about our lives, many of us do things for others all the time without checking in with our bodies and feelings to make sure we are honoring ourselves first. Do you remember a time when you were in a conflict with someone and you were too afraid to communicate your feelings, because you felt intimidated by the way you expected him or her to respond to you? You were more concerned with the other person's reaction than with your own well-being, so you held back your truth. You lodged it somewhere inside your body—maybe in your chest or throat. Maybe you even felt sick. Speaking your truth places you in your power, and it can also help you feel better. Taking the power back by expressing yourself feels liberating.

No one is any better than you. Your success is independent of anyone and anything. Don't feel enslaved to a particular person or situation. If, for example, you are extremely excited about a job interview, be aware that this job is not your only big break. If you don't get it, it just wasn't meant to be right now, and there will be another job for you. The same thing applies when you go out on a first date with someone. If this person is not the answer to your prayers, so be it; there will be someone else who is a better match. Keep a positive attitude, trust in life and in your abilities, and you will draw the right situations and people to you.

Everyone is unique; everyone is connected in the harmonious balance of all things. Admiring good qualities and values in people is healthy, but if we idolize someone, we are creating an inaccurate image of them, which benefits no one. Often, when we really get to know the person we have idolized, we realize that they don't live up to the image we have created, and we are disappointed with ourselves. Indeed, hero worship is a betrayal of loyalty to ourselves, for it means we are not valuing ourselves. Instead, we are assuming that the other person is better than we are: smarter, prettier, funnier, more confident, wiser, more athletic, richer, more intuitive, a better businessperson, a better actor, more artistic, better-looking, more charismatic, more charming, more elegant, more worldly, a better lover, or more creative.

A new situation or relationship can make us feel vulnerable. It's easy to get lost in the excitement of life with new people, new projects, new careers, but it's imperative to stay in your power and not let others manipulate or abuse your time, ideas, or focus. Have the courage to speak your mind, and stay true to who you are. Remember your focus, your agenda, your values. Don't compromise yourself just because you are in unknown territory. It may be unknown for a short time, but only you know yourself and how you want your life to be. If you feel that you're lacking love in any way, this is a good time to connect with yourself and with the divine. Draw your energy back to you by taking some contemplative time. Be more concerned about how you feel than how others feel about you. This is a good time to tell yourself all day long how much you love yourself. Nurture yourself with your favorite healthy foods, comfort clothes, and music; take a walk in nature; go to a prayer garden; play with a puppy or a baby.

A big part of expressing ourselves is through our words. Words are meant to mean something. Words are an expression of our character, of whom we stand for as a person, as an individual in this world. It's important to cherish the words we speak, cherish the ability to have such a mighty impact on others just through our communication. It's a privilege to have that ability. It's best for us to be up front and honest about how we feel, with compassion but without the fear of hurting someone's feelings. It's more responsible to say no than to commit to something and not show up. If we say things to other people because we think that's what they want to hear, or we keep quiet and don't express our truth, we are enabling someone else to believe a lie. This is not authenticity. To feel empowered is to feel authentic. The other person will appreciate your ability to be straightforward. It's far better than saying yes to something you don't want to do. More likely than not, the other person wouldn't want you to do them any favors by saying yes and meaning no, which is insulting to them and is not honoring your integrity.

Dating is another area full of lessons in boundaries, expression, and exploring personal power. If you aren't interested in the other person, it's far better to use honest communication than just not to return someone's calls. You'll feel better because you spoke your truth, and the energy will be clear and clean because he or she isn't wondering about the next date. Don't be afraid to let the person know if they said or did something that offends you. You will feel empowered that you spoke up for yourself. There's nothing wrong with being tactful, but ultimately, honesty is more important than someone's feelings.

Another way we disempower ourselves is by holding on to anger, resentments, or hurts from the past. A client of mine was playing the victim role, still angry and giving her power away to her ex-husband. By making him the bad guy and blaming him for her unhappiness and her life, she kept herself spinning in this anger for several years. On our second coaching session together, I asked if she thought four years was enough time to suffer. I asked her, "What are the greatest things that you've accomplished in the past several years?" She said she never thought she could raise three kids on her own. I told her that was a huge accomplishment and that I saw her as a hero. She was proud of her courage to survive, and she took great pleasure in her close relationship with her children. She was very proud of how self-sufficient she was and of how her kids turned out. She's doing very well today, in a thriving career and much happier.

Another of my clients shared with me that she was emotionally attached to her clients. If they were angry or upset about something, she got upset, and she was emotionally connected to them for years. She had become friends with her clients and wanted to please them, and in the process she had kept the relationships very casual and hadn't created any formal client paperwork. I asked her if she felt that she was operating at the mercy of her clients. She said yes; she would be at their beck and call whenever they needed her, working feverishly in crunch time and even getting anxiety attacks. I asked her if she felt that she was codependent with her clients. She said, yes, but that she hadn't realized it until then. I asked her if she would feel comfortable creating some structure in her business, and she readily agreed. I gave her homework: to create a client profile sheet. She felt comfortable doing that. I also worked with her on not taking on her clients' emotions and not taking personally what they said. It's fine to have friendly relationships with your clients, but it's also important to create boundaries in a professional structure, so that each party knows what is expected; this establishes mutual respect. My client realized that her dependency on her clients was "operating out of fear"—fear of losing her clients. She was trying too hard to keep them happy, at the cost of her own health and happiness.

Taking your power back is really about drawing your energy back into yourself, drawing your love and attention to yourself. It's liberating! The first step is to become aware when you feel depleted, when you feel that too much of your energy is going out and you aren't happy. Ask yourself these questions:

- Do I feel respected, uplifted, and honored?
- Do I feel balanced and relaxed?
- Am I expressing my feelings?
- Am I acting in a way that honors my knowledge, skills, needs, passions or wisdom?

Each situation is different. Only you can determine what is right for you. If you need to take your power back, you have many options. Take a break from the situation or person; communicate your feelings and needs; give yourself the love you need; permanently remove yourself from an unhealthy set of circumstances; leave that dead-end job, career, or relationship and set up healthy boundaries. Love and respect yourself so much that you are confident in what you believe and who you are. Know how important you are in this world and how much you affect others. Feeling powerful is an amazing feeling—it's freedom. You are free to feel powerful just in being you.

Value Who You Are

We place a high importance on values in our life. They are so important to us that we live by them. Values include such things as honesty, loyalty, bravery, diplomacy, integrity, love, kindness, family, a relationship with the divine, affection, the ability to communicate, love of nature, sense of humor, openness to life, trust, responsible, confidence, intelligence, wisdom, acceptance of others, faith, respect, playfulness, adventure, education, security, material wealth, peace, self-expression, balance, freedom, open-mindedness, competitiveness, independence, humanitarianism, centeredness. Living life according to our values brings joy.

Here are some questions to help you explore your relationship with your values. Write your responses to these questions in your journal.

- Whom do you admire most in the world, living or deceased?
- What are the qualities of the people you admire the most?
- What are the five qualities you like the most about yourself?
- When you feel great about your life, describe what that feels like: what you're doing, where you're doing it, and who is around you.
- If you were writing a heartfelt letter to your grandchild, leaving important words of wisdom, what would be your five most important thoughts?

Review your responses from each question, and make a list of the words you used more than once. These are your core values. If you want to remember these core values, write them down in your journal. When you need to make an important decision in your life, you can review your values and ask yourself if your decision will allow you to live life closer or further from your values.

Every time we do something that honors what we believe in, or say something we feel passionate about, our inner light shines. The more we do things we love, we are creating more joy and peace into our lives. Have patience with the process of becoming your own best friend. The universe is designed in perfect order. We have the ability through love and faith to attract our desires to us.

Being honest with yourself and others is vitally important. When we are not honest with others, we are only hurting ourselves, because it means that there is a part of us we don't fully love or that we don't feel strong enough to express something. This dishonesty robs us of our joy. It's important to accept all of who we are, knowing that we continue to learn and strive to be the best we can be, which is all we can do. Being dishonest means we are not happy with some part of who we are. It means we think we are supposed to be better, do better, or look better in some way. The next time you feel tempted to lie, ask yourself, "Why do I have to create a lie or a story about something? What part of myself am I not accepting?

Value yourself first, and you will automatically value others. How you treat yourself is how you treat others. Every spirit is so unique, special, and gifted, it's no mistake that you are here. Your light is absolutely needed in the orchestration of this divine universe. Your soul and spirit uplift many people who come into contact with you, though you are not even aware of it. Peel away the internal chatter—our mental "graffiti"—and allow your light to shine brighter yet.

Have you ever noticed how some people are different in the beginning of a relationship? They seem to act in a way that they think the other person wants them to act. They become what they think the other person wants. Then, years later, they go their separate ways, both of them disappointed because they think the other person "changed." Have the love and courage to be who you are. You don't want to be with someone who doesn't accept you for who you are, anyway. Don't you deserve to be accepted, loved, and adored for being you? I remember meeting a guy and thinking immediately that he was so great, I got a bit nervous. Later that night I asked myself, "What was that all about? I don't even know this person." I was making assumptions. The next day I met him for lunch, and (surprise!) he was not what I expected, and I never did see him again. A lesson learned again. My focus was on him, wondering what he thinks about me. My focus should be on how I felt about him. And it takes time to really get to know someone. He needed to impress me, and not the other way around.

The divine does not limit us; we limit ourselves. Begin to think and believe bigger for yourself. You may be holding on to an old memory of how you thought you were in a past situation, and you still believe that's how you are now. If you can recognize these images, you can then create more uplifting, positive ones to replace them. Sometimes in life we get accustomed to things not going our way, or people not treating us how we feel we should be treated, and before long that is what we expect. Start thinking about everything working out for you. Feel worthy of everything working out. Change your programming. Begin to think bigger for yourself. Begin to treat yourself with the same amount of love the divine has for you—unconditional love. The more you grow in your own love, the greater the possibilities, and the greater the love you can give to others.

Not Caring What Other People Think

Our human nature wants others to like us. But we don't want to care so much that we compromise ourselves by not being relaxed, comfortable, and confident. The more we allow our passions, joy, and light to shine, the more the entire universe benefits. I come across people who hide their spiritual beliefs because they are afraid of what their families or friends may think. This is an example of dimming your light and not speaking your truth. When you compromise your values and beliefs to the point that it's hurting your spirit, you're denying the core of who you are. Don't allow others to take you off your path. Don't allow other people's fears to penetrate into your world. A peaceful life comes from following and believing in your dreams, walking to the beat of your own drum, and not conforming to what others want and expect. Have faith in yourself and in the universal power of divine love. This is where freedom lies—freedom to be yourself. Choose the things you want to do. Choose to be you and not someone else. Life is short, and you can't get time back. Try to live your life without caring so much what others think. Instead, ask yourself, "Why do I care what other people think?" I use these words quite often, and they work. I immediately take a deep breath, visualize taking my power back, and relax.

Pay attention to when your spirit is hurting; it's a sure sign that you're not honoring yourself. Love yourself so much that you aren't afraid what anyone thinks, especially the people closest to you. Family, friends, coworkers, acquaintances can pass their judgments and fears along to you. Be careful that you don't change your life to accommodate others. If you are being triggered on a deep level by the comments you are receiving from people you respect, this may be an opportunity for you to reevaluate your feelings and beliefs and see if there is any validity to what you're hearing. Look at the "sting" inside the words. Maybe healing needs to happen that isn't yet complete.

Once you take responsibility through awareness, you can ask the divine to help you bring light and truth to this belief or this newly uncovered part of you. For example, your lifelong friend tells you that your behavior can be very controlling at times. Instead of getting defensive, becoming a victim by displaying behavior of being hurt, or responding back in a dramatic way, spend quiet time to see if there are times when you have been controlling. Ask the divine to show you the truth. Sincerely ask your friend to give you examples so you are clear about what he or she is saying. Take responsibility for your actions. Once you can own this, you can learn and grow from it.

Personalizing a situation means we are telling ourselves that something occurred because of us. We make the story about us by assuming that we did something wrong or that we are the cause— maybe not good enough or not worthy in some way. We are now hurt even though, in most cases, what someone else does has nothing to do with us. The other person is making choices based on his or her life experiences. We are responsible for our own happiness, and taking the blame for someone else's actions isn't necessarily an empowering reaction. You are the master of your heart, body, and spirit, not your neighbor, coworker, boss, relative, friend, or acquaintance. If you really want to know what someone thinks, ask the divine.

> *Fear knocked at the door. Love answered and no one was there.*
> —Ancient proverb—

Forgiveness

It's important for our health and well-being to forgive everyone in our lives who has hurt us in some way. When we forgive people we are allowing this sadness, anger, hurt, betrayal, and loss to leave our body and release us of the anguish and pain. Forgiveness does not mean we condone the behavior; it does not mean we must have a relationship with the person who hurt us. Forgiveness means we take our power back. Forgiveness means we are choosing not to focus on the hurt any longer. Focusing on the hurt now is keeping us connected to the past. Holding on to this energy is keeping us shaded from our own light. Forgiveness is a big part of self-love. Because we love ourselves so much, we understand the importance of freeing ourselves of past hurts. Letting go of the past brings our energy back to us to live in the present. We are not allowing our memories of the past to hold us captive. We are not allowing another person to have power over us anymore. We are able to live a more peaceful and empowered life.

When we reach adulthood, we can choose to release unhappy memories by seeing the growth in those experiences. Those situations aid us in some way in our life. They may make you a stronger person or give you more compassion. See the situation from a higher perspective; change your perception and, by doing so, make it easier for you to let it go. Allow the situation to release from your body, spirit, and mind. You are ready to love yourself more; this is freedom. If "forgive" is too strong a word for you to use in certain life situations, than make a conscious decision just to let the emotions go, let the pain go. Just tell yourself it's time to let all that go, and let it go with the highest vibration of love surrounding the situation. Ask the divine to come into your heart and help you release the situation. If you have to do this many times, it's okay; God won't get bored. Trust in your heart that these experiences have assisted with your spiritual growth.

Take out a piece of paper or write these exercises in your journal:

A. Sit quietly to get clear on what is upsetting you. Write out your feelings. Where is the anger and hurt coming from? Do you have expectations of another person? Are you personalizing a situation?

Get in a comfortable position, close your eyes, and relax all the muscles in your body. Begin to connect with your breath, bringing the breath all the way down to your abdomen. Invite the divine and the highest vibration of love to surround you. Invite the divine to enter your heart. Invite your higher self in. Imagine a pure white light surrounding you. If you choose, you can invite in the higher wisdom of the person you are in conflict with. Say whatever you need to say to this person to clear your heart. Ask this person's higher wisdom any questions you may have. Listen, and trust any intuitive information that you are receiving. Allow all your emotions to come out. If you want to, imagine the other person saying what they need to say back to you. Notice whether you feel lighter. Maybe you're both apologizing and smiling at each other. Imagine the energy between the two of you as being healed, and notice how you're feeling. Maybe you hug each other. Ask this person to give you back any of your power that you gave to them. Visualize your power coming back through the transmission of white light. Thank this person's wiser self for participating in this forgiveness exercise. Bless them. Notice whether you feel lighter. Also notice if there's anything you need to forgive yourself for.

B. Read this list out loud, and then write it in your journal.

"I release _____ (insert name), and all anger, hurt, and blame."

"I am focusing on forgiveness, joy, peace, and love."

"I am living in the present."

"I am healed and free."

I believe that before we incarnate on earth, we choose our parents and siblings to assist us with our life plan and life lessons. Imagine, for example, that if we are meant to learn self-love in this lifetime, our parents may have gifted us with lessons that challenged us to love ourselves when we didn't feel loved by them.

I believe that family is very important. If more people can put down their grudges and call their family members—daughter, son, mom, dad, brother, or sister—and just say, "I love you," the world will feel a great sense of relief. It doesn't matter who's right or wrong, who's different, who is from the old school of doing things, who calls whom more, who does more in the family—just love them anyway. In situations involving wrongdoings, pray for healing, love, compassion, and abundance for your family members.

If we really want love, we must learn how to forgive.
—Mother Teresa—

Many people harbor bad feelings toward their parents for one reason or another. Through my observation, many people compare their parents against their friends' parents and create expectations of what and how parents should be and what parents should do for them, buy for them, and give to them. These are unfair expectations to place on parents. There is no guidebook that says that in order to be a good parent you must give your children a certain amount of money, pay for everything until they are married, and be at their beck and call. These are judgments of how we think parents should be. Our parents gave us life. They wiped our eyes and noses when we cried, changed our diapers, and fed us. This doesn't mean that we must agree with everything our parents do. It doesn't even mean we have to like who they are now, but we send love and blessings to them and honor their life path.

It's important to take inventory and see if we are harboring any ill will toward ourselves that can be released. Throughout our lives, we may harbor feelings of anger, guilt, disappointment, shame, and judgment. Choosing to release these emotions through forgiveness will free us. Each moment you think of yourself in an old light is a moment you're still living in the past. You can also choose to change the way you view your past. Why not view it in a more empowering way that can help you make peace and move on?

Observe how you describe major events in your life. An acquaintance of mine was expressing how dreadful his divorce was. If he were to focus on what he learned from that relationship, I wonder whether he would describe his divorce differently and have an easier time forgiving. Relationships are in our life to help us grow into our own acceptance of our divine nature.

Here is a powerful inner-child forgiveness meditation. If this is a new exercise for you, please consider hiring a coach or counselor to support you through the process.

Gather pictures of yourself as a child at different ages. Place the pictures in front of you and take a look at yourself. Sit comfortably or lie down, close your eyes, breathe, and relax all your muscles. Visualize your inner child—that little person inside you, or what you look like in one of the pictures in front of you. Notice how he or she feels. What does this child look like? How old? Is he or she scared, sad, happy, joyful, excited? What is the child doing? Is he or she close to you? Do you feel connected to your inner child? Ask the child what it needs from you? Trust whatever information comes up. Tell him or her that you will always be there and that they can rely on you. See yourself playing with your inner child. Tell her or him that they don't need to look outward for approval or validation. Tell the child you are sorry if you were not there as you should have been or if you didn't give them the love they needed. Give the child a hug; wipe away their tears. Let them know you will be more reliable now and will check in with them on a more frequent basis. Tell them they are very important to you and that you will never leave them. Notice whether the child trusts you. Visualize green light going from your heart to theirs. Tell him or her that you will never go away, you are reliable, and you will check in with them every day.

Following Your Heart's Desire

Following your heart puts you on a path with many rewards and gifts. It is a path that brings you closer to who you are and allows you to express your passions. You learn to trust yourself, trust your intuition, and trust life and the divine. After making one of the biggest decisions in your life, which is a mighty leap of faith into the abyss of the unknown, your mind will likely be filled with agonizing questions. How am I going to pay the bills? How do I build my dream career and get business? Am I going to be any good at this? Your faith, determination, and courage may be challenged every step of the way. But if you stay true to your spirit, with patience, you will keep moving ahead. It's a strong sense of inner knowing that will propel you forward. You may not understand fully, but it will feel right. When you get beyond the fears, what's waiting for you is the gift of love, faith, and inner peace.

You have chosen to love yourself more than your fears and more than other people's fears for you. You have chosen to live in harmony with your spirit. You may have made some sacrifices: eaten out less, cut back on major purchases, done your own house cleaning, canceled the cable movie stations, stopped taking expensive vacations and buying expensive holiday gifts. And in time you reap the rewards. You learn to be patient with yourself and your life process. You learn that the world is in divine order, and as you grow more comfortable and self-assured in your new role, your new business grows. You are learning along the way, laughing at yourself, and enjoying the process. You learn to release what is no longer useful, in order to allow for the new that awaits just around the corner. By not clinging so tightly to how you think your life should look, you learn to hold space for a higher vision. You begin to get excited because things are starting to come together, things are falling into place; more people desire your services or products. You are appreciative and grateful to be enjoying every day doing what you love. Your light is shining, and everyone around you can feel it. The world is benefiting by you being you and doing what you love.

And I believe that everyone can have this fulfillment and excitement—just listen to your heart. It will call out to you in many ways, and it's important to trust what you're hearing and feeling. It reminds you of what you have forgotten, what you've been ignoring, what you agreed to come here to do. Hold on to your strong belief in abundance, for this will help you have faith that you will be successful in following your heart. The universe has enough money and opportunities for you to be successful if that is truly what you desire. This is the path to success.

I encourage anyone who is truly interested in experiencing greater fulfillment to get busy and follow your heart's desire. The whole world benefits when we follow your heart, because only then are you happy. When you are not living life authentically, it doesn't benefit anyone. You can express your passion as a hobby or special interest, something you do in your free time; it doesn't necessarily mean that you quit your job and do something else immediately, unless, of course, that is what you are guided to do. If you are at a stage where you want to do something different in your life but don't know how to do it and pay your bills at the same time, you have much in common with a great many people. Here are some questions that will help you determine just what your heart's desire really is:

- What activities bring you great joy?
- If you were eighty years old and reviewing your life, what would you wish you had done?
- What subjects fascinate you?
- What kinds of workshops or events do you enjoy attending?
- If you had enough money and didn't have to work, what would you do to occupy your time?
- If you were in "heaven, or "the spirit realm," right now, living in love, what would you want to do?
- What are your hobbies?
- What do you enjoy talking about? A good clue is to recall conversations when your voice was vibrant and you were talking with enthusiasm and passion.
- What was your major or electives in college? What did you do as your college internships and jobs?
- What did you do as a child when you were playing?
- What kinds of awards did you receive when you were younger?
- What are the suggestions you receive from other people about what you are good at doing?
- Do you want to be part of a small, medium, or large company?
- Do you want to create your own business?
- Are you self-motivated, interested in working from home?

- How much time to do allow yourself with the things that are important to you?
- Do you feel guilt when you do the things that you love if they don't bring you money?
- If you were granted three wishes, what would they be?

Listen to the guidance from your heart, not just your head. Trust that the universe will provide for you. As you go through your daily life, become genuinely aware of the things you like and don't like. This will give you clues about what you want to do and what you like to do. Begin expressing your desires, from the small things, like what you want to eat for dinner or what movie you want to rent, to bigger things, like how you want to decorate your house or where you want to go on vacation. Keep it up, and soon you will be living authentically, following your heart and living through your heart in all ways. Have patience, trust life, and remember to breathe.

Formula for following your heart:
1. Meditate.
2. Pray. Ask the divine for help, and then listen. Here's a prayer for guidance and support: "Infinite Intelligence, please give concrete direction to my life path and help me stay focused in the best and highest direction for my life purpose."
3. Write your intentions on paper. (Further detailed in chapter 3)
4. Review your beliefs about your intention; notice if there are any fears that need to be transmuted.
5. Create a plan of action. Identify what you want, how you want it, who's involved, why you want to do this, where you want to be. List the action steps to take to make this happen. Write out your goals for the week, six months and a year.
6. Designate a specific time of day to do one thing to move forward in your desired direction. Don't allow distractions to take you away from this commitment.

7. Figure out how you will pay the bills in the meantime. Can you borrow money? Get a part-time job? Sell an investment? Refinance? Cut down on expenses? Put yourself on a budget?

8. Research opportunities on the Internet in your area (or possibly other areas).

9. Is there another place you've always wanted to live?

10. Read books in your desired field.

11. Write e-mails to people who are already successful in your field. Ask how they got started, and ask for contacts, advertising, and promotional avenues that worked for them.

12. Send a note of thanks to anyone who helps you.

13. Attend networking functions in your field of interest; network with your current friends and business associates.

14. Call the chamber of commerce. They usually sell a directory of businesses in a particular city.

15. Go to the library and read the newspaper of the city you may want to move to.

16. Pursue any certifications or degrees necessary in your field.

17. Follow the flow. Observe what and who flows into your life, and how.

18. Most important, begin doing what you want to do in whatever capacity presents itself, even offering a service for free.

Take one day at a time and focus on your interest. The good thing is, if this is your calling, once you make the decision to take action and move forward in that direction, the universe will support you. Imagine your plan like a ball of clay that can be molded and redirected as needed.

Put your full attention on any project you're working on. This will keep you present and focused on your main intent. Think about all the various projects you have going, and ask yourself, "Why am I doing it?" Have more fun in the process: learn, create, open yourself up. This will keep you grounded in the moment. You don't want to miss it. That way, when it's all done, you'll always remember your enjoyment, and that's the real treasure. It's not just about getting to the finish line; it's every tiny step getting there.

At times the divine may have to take big measures to keep you on your life path. For example, if, even though you're miserable, you stay in a job too long because you fear the loss of money or your children's medical insurance, watch out! You may get fired. The divine, will do what's necessary to get you to where you need to be to stay on your life path. I was fired, and it turned out to be the best thing for my life and career. The same goes if you're staying in an unhealthy relationship too long. If you're not going to listen to your heart, the divine may have to do something extravagant to get you out of that relationship. Avoid the pain and drama; listen to your heart and take forward action. When your heart is filled with gratitude, joy, and love, the entire world benefits.

Visualization

This meditation is for any situation in your life where doubts, fears, or worries may come up — career issues, health-related issues, relationships, or anything else.

The heart is the place of truth. It is not a place where doubts or worries can reside. Unlike our minds, it doesn't allow our exaggerated thoughts to get in the way. It is the place of only truth.

1. Inhale and exhale out of the mouth with a really big sigh, letting everything go.
2. Place your hands over your heart, breathe into your heart. Notice how your heart feels.
3. Bring your situation in with your breath into your heart. Whatever it is you're questioning — career, health issue, love life, or anything else.
4. What is your heart telling you? What is the essence of what it wants?

5. Ask your heart, "What is the truth in this situation?" What is your heart telling you about this situation?

6. Bring all your senses into the situation while you're exploring the situation in your heart. What does this feel like? Look like? What are you hearing or smelling?

7. Trust all images, thoughts, feelings, and impressions coming up for you. Write them down. Breathe out the doubt with your exhalation.

8. Exhale _____(insert doubt here). Inhale _____ (insert the truth you're hearing or the outcome you desire).

Intention Exercise

I intend to bask in my own love.

I intend to do something today that honors my desires.

I intend to be courageous!

Prayer

I ask for help to release and forgive others and myself for any perceived wrongdoings.

May all beings know their own value and authentically express themselves.

I pray to be connected to my divine nature.

Joy Journal

Write about how you honored your values today. What did you do or say that was in line with what is important to you? When have you used and trusted your intuition in life? How did it benefit you or others? Write about when you feel strong and empowered in your life. What are you doing?

Gratitude Journal

Write about all the things you have done in your life that you are grateful for and that ended up benefiting you or others. Who has come into your life and been a blessing in disguise, and why is this so? What moment in your life are you most grateful for, and why?

Affirmation

I feel my connection to the divine

I trust my intuition.

I am a forgiving, loving person.

Request

1. Write a forgiveness letter to yourself or someone else. Release this letter by burning it, mailing it, or throwing it away.

2. Begin doing something that your heart is calling out for — using your creative abilities, starting a new project, or whatever it may be.

Chapter 3
Co-creating Your Life

You are co-creating with the universe with every thought, feeling, emotion, and word. Each thought carries its own unique vibration that attracts the same vibration to you. This is how you're creating your own world. You are creating in every moment. You are that powerful!

With awareness, we have the power to choose to create more positive experiences than we can even imagine, through the universal law of attraction. What we think about, we draw to us. Thought is vibration. These vibrations attract to us thoughts of other people, situations, and circumstances that resonate at the same frequency. Our eyes can't see these energy waves. If we continue the same thought for a long time or if the thought is very strong, the speed of our manifestation is quicker. This goes for positive and negative thoughts. How do you feel, knowing you have so much more power than you ever thought possible in creating your life? You may be thinking, "That's a scary thought!" But now that you know how it works, you can make conscious choices about what you think and speak about.

You can observe your emotions and see if they are in line with your desires. You may have heard the saying "Where our attention goes, our energy flows." We choose what we hold in our consciousness. Therefore, we choose what we're creating in our lives. Every action and thought has an effect or consequence. If it's a positive thought, then the effect will be positive. We have the power to positively help other people with our thoughts, too. For example, let's say your neighbor desperately wants to sell her home, but time is going by and she's not getting any offers. She begins to get discouraged because the realtors are telling her it's a really bad time to try to sell a home. Feeling sympathy for your neighbor, you could join in with "Oh, it's such a terrible time to sell now; there are so many homes for sale and no one is buying or selling anything; you'd better drop the sale price." Or you could envision new neighbors living next door to you. Hold the knowing that your neighbor's home will sell to the right person at the right time. If she really wants to move, tell her to envision herself packing her boxes and moving to her new neighborhood. We don't have to buy into the mass consciousness of fear, or what's going on in the news or the marketplace. Hold the energy and vision that anything is possible.

Without using words, through our thoughts and feelings, we contribute energetically to situations all the time. Our thoughts are energy. This energy goes out into the universe and carries a vibration. The more sensitive we become to energy, the more we can sense these thoughts. As an example, let's say your friend informs you that she cheated on her husband with a much younger guy. You're trying to be a good listener without judging her, but as you're listening, your thoughts are saying, "Oh, my God, I can't believe she cheated on her husband. Something must be unstable in their home." All of a sudden, your friend picks up on your thoughts and feels your discord. She responds, asking if you think she's wrong or if you're passing judgment on her. Whether words are spoken or not, we must take responsibility even for our unspoken energy, In many cases this is what people are sensing anyway. In this situation, the energy was felt accurately. Our thought forms are very powerful.

In the book *The Hidden Messages in Water*, Dr. Emoto has proved how powerful feelings, words, and thoughts affect the universe. The proof is in his photographs of water samples. These samples show the effects of focused spoken words, unspoken words, and music presented to the same water samples. Dr. Emoto found crystals formed in frozen water changed. Water from clear springs exposed to kind, loving words showed beautiful, clear, and amazing snowflake structures. The water exposed to negative thoughts, words, and commands were muddy, disconnected, and without any structure. It is very fascinating and powerful to see the extreme difference in the pictures of the crystallized water.

Dr. Emoto goes on to say, "The implications of this research create a new awareness of how we can positively impact the earth and our personal health." He says, "Science of quantum mechanics generally acknowledges that substance is nothing more than vibration. The entire universe is in a state of vibration, and each thing generates its own frequency."

Our mental health affects not only water but our physical health, too. In the book *Healing with the Mind's Eye*, the author speaks about the "Indian parable about a man who sees a snake in the road and experiences all of the sensations of terror: his heartbeat speeds up, his palms become sweaty, and he gets butterflies in his stomach. After his initial freight, the man realizes the object of his terror in the road is not a snake at all but a rope lying coiled in road. He breathes a sigh of relief and relaxes. His heart rate drops, his breathing slows down, and his stomach returns to normal. What the mind thinks is real, it's real to this person, and the body's physiology changes in response." What we think and feel affects our body.

Since it's imperative to understand how our mental health affects our lives, I listen to people's language everywhere I go. I can see how their language is creating their life. I have said for many years now, it's time for a "New Language," a new way to see the world, a new way to perceive things. A language of beauty in a world where we recognize miracles as normal occurrences. A language based on love, gratitude, compassion, synchronicity, faith, a deep understanding of our connectedness to everyone, everything, and the divine.

If spirit should take a snapshot of your thoughts, are they serving your higher good or the higher good of others around you? You are creating your own life with every thought and feeling. While teaching hatha yoga, I hear students' comments such as, "Oh, I can't do that," before they have even tried it, and yet they are so quick to judge themselves instead of just appreciating wherever they are in a pose.

If we focus and concentrate more on the positive things and more empowering thoughts, on what we want, on the things that are working, that is what expands. Let's say you're beginning a new business and you have a few customers. Instead of focusing on the lack of business, focus on really appreciating your two clients. This energy will attract more clients. A big part of this is also believing in your own ability.

We can do this creative imagery for any situation. Wherever we place energy with our thoughts, feelings, beliefs, and perceptions, that is what we are increasing. So if we are focusing on love, compassion, joy, blessings, and gratitude, that is what we are attracting to us. Can you imagine how powerful collective prayer or collective thought is?

In the book *Healing with the Mind's Eye*, the author cites a study from W. Harris at the Mid America Heart Institute, Saint Luke's Hospital in Kansas City, Missouri. In this study, the objective was to determine whether remote, intercessory prayer for hospitalized cardiac patients will reduce overall adverse events and length of stay.

He conducted a random, controlled trial of the effects of remote, intercessory prayer on outcomes in patients admitted to the coronary care unit. Nine hundred ninety consecutive patients who were newly admitted to the coronary unit were randomized to receive remote, intercessory prayer, or just the usual treatment. The first names of the patients in the prayer group were given to a team of outside intercessors who prayed for them daily for four weeks. The intercessors didn't know the patients and the patients were unaware they anyone was praying for them. The research conclusions were that remote, intercessory prayer was associated with lower coronary care unit complication and incident scores. The result was that prayer was an effective adjunct to standard medical care. Patients who were prayed for had less complications and did better.

Throughout most of your day, do your thoughts and emotions bring you peace and joy? I read somewhere that if we were to write down our thoughts at the end of each day we would be surprised that we have an average of over 300 negative comments that spin around in our minds every day. With my yoga students I refer to this as our "internal graffiti." Begin to be aware of your internal graffiti.

Step 1

The first step is to be aware. Catch yourself when you are about to use a derogatory term such as stupid, idiot, fool, weirdo, loser, moron, jerk, dumb, ugly, fool, or when using phrases such as "I can't afford that," "I can't do this," "I'm not deserving, can't trust people, haven't got a chance," "What's the use? Nobody cares," "It will be too tough to do this," "My work isn't anything special," "Things are just getting worse," "It's not going to work out the way I want," "No one likes me," "Life is a grind," "I can't win," "You can't trust anyone," "They're all crazy," or "I'm not smart enough or good enough to do that." Here's a pet peeve of mine: When you ask someone if they can do something and they respond, "Not a problem" or "No problem," why even mention the word "problem" if it's not a problem? Why begin with "Not" when you mean yes? Don't you think this sounds better? "I would love to take care of that for you," or "I'll do it right now," or "That's okay, take your time."

When you are experiencing negative emotions, take a moment to go within and discern the meaning and truth of what you're experiencing. Is your emotion in line with your desire? Ask yourself if the thought you're having is true. Ask if you need validation from others or if it's something you can give to yourself. Ask yourself if you're looking at the situation in the most uplifting way.

You can always ask the divine to assist you in the process. If you are angry inside, spend a moment discerning where this anger is coming from. Is it covering up an area in your life where you are hurt or sad?

Step 2

The next step is to choose to let it go and change our thoughts and emotions. Tell yourself that you are in charge of your thoughts and that you're going to change your thoughts and emotions. The more you practice this, the more quickly you will catch yourself spinning and will stop sending out this negative energy.

These tiny little sayings have a way of creeping into our minds, and if we catch them early enough, we can shine white light on them and envision in big letters the word CANCEL in your mind.

Step 3

Visualize exactly what you desire. Allow the feeling and emotions of what you desire to bubble up inside you. The longer and more frequently you can hold those thoughts, feelings, and emotions, the more intense the energy will be. Here are some empowering thoughts:

- Everything always works out; my persistence pays off; my solution already exists.
- My journey is much more important than my goal.
- The world appreciates me; money always flows in.
- I trust that my projects will succeed; abundance is everywhere.
- I always make smart decisions; I draw miracles to me.
- I'm a very lucky person; life is wonderful; I am love.
- Friends are loyal and trustworthy; I'm creative.
- God's love is inside my heart; I love everyone; life is magical.
- Today is a great day; my presence uplifts others.
- I appreciate everyone; I'm in the right place at the right time.
- People are kind everywhere I go; there is always time for the things I'm meant to do!

Many years ago I was in a quiet space, asking my spirit guides a question about personal growth. I asked specifically to be shown where I hold myself back in my own life. They showed me my questions of doubt and feelings of not being good enough. I noticed that I did have those thoughts at times. "I don't think they liked me. They didn't say good-bye; they must not have liked the class. Will they come back? Will anyone want to participate in the workshop? Will they call me back for coaching?"

The message I received was something like this: Stop all the questioning, wondering, and doubting yourself. Stop questioning your validity. Stop questioning your abilities as a teacher. Accept yourself now as a good teacher. Know that you are helping others by just being you—by caring, by sharing your passion and heart. Stop wondering if the students like you. Focus on your own enjoyment.

Are you enjoying yourself? Are you having fun? How do you feel when you're doing it? If you're enjoying yourself, don't worry about anything else. Keep doing the things you enjoy.

I've observed that many people are not even aware of how negative they are. They don't comprehend what a negative thought is compared with a positive thought. They haven't had the conditioning or experience to help them begin to change their thoughts and perceptions. They are creating this type of world for themselves and don't even realize it. All they have to do is change how they look at life.

Here is a process for seeing the world in an uplifting way:

1. Pray for help to see the world through the eyes of the divine.

2. Begin each day with the intention of looking for the beauty in everything and drawing the frequency of abundance to you. Stop yourself if you are noticing more negative things. You can think of it as a game and even play it with your kids, friends, and spouse. You can tell your children and family that the person who lasts the longest saying only positive comments wins something.

3. When you take your very first step outside, stop. Look up at the sky and notice how beautiful it is. Thank the sky and say, "I love you." Then look at a tree and do the same thing. You can exchange energy with the tree. If you see a neighbor, smile and say good morning. Take a few deep belly breaths and begin your day.

4. Bring your neighbors' newspaper up to their door.

5. Sit inside your car; tell you car how much you love it. If you don't like your car, then maybe you are planning on getting a new one fairly soon. Thank your car anyway for all the places it has taken you.

6. Bless the slow driver in front of you for teaching you patience.

7. Thank all the green lights you're getting along your journey.

8. Appreciate the paved roads that are allowing you to have a smooth ride.

9. Appreciate your parking angels for assisting you with a great parking space.

10. Bless your place of business for providing you with the ability to create, expand yourself, make friends, share your creativity, feed your family, pay your bills, and give presents to family, friends and yourself.

11. Look for all the things that help you in achieving your tasks. Thank the copying machine for making your copies successfully; thank the mail carrier for delivering your contracts and checks; thank your assistant for helping you; thank all the people who do anything for you.

12. Thank the bank for keeping your money safe.

13. Appreciate how quickly and timely things get done for you. Put a lot of attention on these things that go really well in your life.

14. Thank your computer and printer and telephone.

15. Believe that the kind and compassionate people and acts in the world far outweigh the negative.

16. Take short breaks throughout your day to breathe, commune with spirit, and stretch your body.

17. Call a friend or loved one to express your love and support.

18. Look at all the beautiful colors in nature as you drive home.

19. When paying your bills, bless them and be thankful for what you have received in return.

20. Use "please" and "thank you" everywhere you go.

21. Bless the slow drivers, and bless the fast drivers. Maybe the slow driver helped you to slow down and avoid a speeding ticket, and maybe the fast driver got the ticket instead of you.

22. Listen to music and feel alive.

We are constant creators. Through our free will that the divine granted us, we choose what type of energy we want to live in. We know that our thoughts can help or hinder us in our lives. Knowing that everything is vibration, we can also extend our thoughts, feelings, and language to objects such as our homes, cars, computers, water, food, electrical appliances, projects, and pretty much anything else by blessing them and sending love and appreciation to them. Before each meal, hold your hands over your food and send love and appreciation into your meal. Allow the vibration between the food and you to integrate. Bless the earth for growing the vegetables, grains, nuts, and fruits, and bless the animal's spirit of the meat, foul, or fish you're eating. And thank the divine for the nutrients that are now blessing and healing your body.

If our hearts are pure, kind, gentle, appreciative, trusting, and peaceful, then that is what kind of world we live in. We must clean up our insides to clean up the external world. War and natural disasters are an indication of our internal struggles, of the war within us.

Beliefs

What we believe is what we create for ourselves. We design and operate our lives based on what we believe. We carry an attitude connected to our belief system. If we believe that everything always works out in life, we will carry that attitude of faith, which draws a peaceful energy to us. If we believe that people are dishonest, we will be apt to attract experiences of dishonesty. If we believe that most people are friendly and helpful, we will attract friendly and helpful people. If we have the courage to go after our dreams, the universe will support us. If we believe that all the good men or woman are taken and that it's impossible to find a mate, then we only make it more difficult to find our partners. If we are open to new possibilities, then we will draw to ourselves new opportunities. If we believe in miracles, we open the doors to them. If we believe that people are out to get us, we may experience getting taken advantage of, or we may have a hard time with intimacy or getting close to people. If we believe that all rich people are snobs, the well-off people we see are likely to be snobs, or we may hinder wealth from coming into our lives. If we have a healthy belief system about money and wealth, we will draw more money to ourselves. If we believe that we must protect ourselves from being hurt by others, we will carry around a shield of armor that keeps people away from us. We carry our beliefs with us wherever we go, not even aware of most of them until we explore them.

Take inventory of your beliefs; some of them may not be serving you. You can make the decision to look at the beliefs that are holding you back from achieving your desires. For example, you may want a new partner in your life, but you may have a belief that all women cheat or that a girlfriend will bring nothing but pain and heartache. These beliefs can hinder that new person from entering your life. Say, for example, you've been praying for a new job and are concerned why you don't have one. Explore what you really believe about getting a good job. Maybe you have a hidden belief that you really won't find a better job, or you have a deep-seated belief that you're really not qualified for anything better, or you're afraid of a new place or fear that you won't find a job that will pay you enough money. Figure out what your hidden beliefs are around your desires; this is very important in helping you reach your desires. If you feel you aren't smart enough, classy enough, worldly enough, or intellectual enough, you may be attracting situations in your life to prove what you believe. Believe more in you. This will open up more opportunities.

Look at all the parts of your life where you are unhappy and want to be different. Also, look at the areas you're pleased with. These are clues to how you can explore what you really believe in all areas of your life. Then take an inventory of your beliefs. Find out if you have any subtle, hidden belief that is holding you back from what you think you desire. Or maybe what you think you desire isn't accurate.

Here's an exercise to explore your beliefs in all areas of your life. Take out your journal and write your responses to the questions below. Allow yourself to write whatever feels natural to you. On a scale of one to ten, ten being the highest, how would you rate where you feel you stand in each area? Ask yourself what you truly believe in these areas of your life:

- What is your current belief about wealth and money?
- What is your current belief about romance and sex, and how does your spouse or partner fit in?
- What is your current belief about your intuition?
- What is your current belief about your career?
- What is your current belief about your self-development?
- What is your current belief about family and friendships?
- What is your current belief about physical health and your body?
- What are your current beliefs about organized religion and spirit?
- What are your current beliefs about your life purpose?

Notice I use the word "current" with each of these beliefs. It's important to take a moment and check whether you really believe something or whether you are just parroting an old belief that no longer applies to you. When you have completed the exercise, begin working on any area of your life upon which you would like to focus. Put more of your daily energy and attention in that direction to create change or growth.

Do your beliefs support your desires? Is there inner work to be done first to change or clarify your beliefs? Write them all down. Then, to the right of each, write down a new positive belief that supports your true desires. An example follows.

Undesired Beliefs	Desired Beliefs
I'm not intuitive.	I am putting more time into sensing energy, and I've noticed that I have become much more intuitive. I'm sensing that my friend needs help managing her time and energy.
Tall people get more.	I'm the perfect size and shape for my life's purpose. My body is an external representation supporting me on my life journey.

In a visualization, allow white light to cleanse away the old beliefs that don't support you. See them as melting away or dissolving from your cells and draining out the soles of your feet. Give your body permission to release. Hold the intention that they are gone. You can also use the white light as little bombs, blowing the old beliefs up. Then imagine your new beliefs inside your cells. Create an image of what your life would be like with your new beliefs. How do you feel with these new beliefs? What is your life like? How are you benefiting?

Honor your desires by taking time to break them down and explore what you really believe. Your desires are manifestations of your thoughts and beliefs. Breathe in your affirmations three hundred times a day until these literally become your beliefs. You are sending these thoughts to your subconscious mind. Your subconscious mind listens to your conscious mind. The power is within *you* to create a more harmonious, peaceful, empowered life. Say your affirmations out loud, and truly believe them. Your affirmations must be believable to you, so that you're sending out authentic energy.

Believe in yourself; believe that your dreams are easily ascertained and that you deserve them and more. Continue to trust and have faith while you're living fully engaged in every moment. Believe that anything is possible. Breathe and smile. Have patience and observe where you are putting your focus. Don't give up before the miracle occurs.

> *We change our biology with our beliefs.*
> —Deepak Chopra—

If you ever want a good picture of what is going on inside you, look at your external world. It's as if the universe were videotaping you all the time. As you learn to embody more of what you want, you will draw more of that same frequency to you. For example, if you want more joy in your life, think about your most joyous moments and remember how you feel when you are joyful and doing joyful things. The energy vibration of joy is powerful; this will attract the same vibration back to you, bringing you more joyful experiences.

What does love feel like to you? Remember how you have felt on your birthday, your wedding day, or any special day or time in your life. Think about the energy vibration of feeling special and loved— that feeling of happiness and joy—and breathe that into your whole being. That energy will be transmitted out into the universe and will attract a similar vibration to you. Whatever quality you're looking for, be its essence and allow it to fill every cell in your body.

If you are sending out a "needy" vibration, the universe will give you lessons that allow you to see just where you're giving your power away. In my past relationships, I was searching for love outside myself; therefore, the men in my life were treating me in a way that clearly mirrored my neediness. I stopped attracting those particular situations when I increased my self-love. This is just another of the many situations where my external world was mirroring my internal world. If you become what you want, you will receive more of what you have come to embody.

If we want money, we don't want to put too much energy on not having it. That just draws more life situations to us that prove to us that we don't have money. Keep the focus on appreciating every paycheck, every purchase you were able to make, and every penny found on the street. Use language such as "I am a money magnet; I walk around and attract wealth everywhere I go." Observe whether you make derogatory comments about people who have money. Observe how you feel around wealth. If you are uncomfortable, this energy may keep money away from you. If you want more friends, be a friend to others and be your own best friend. It's important that these intentions be sent out with a sense of honesty, detachment, and love.

Creating Intentions

Setting your intentions is a wonderful way to get clear on what you truly desire, and to allow the energy of your desires to attract to you exactly what you want. Focus on how you want to feel, what you want to do, and what you want to have. Imagine the best result. When you awake in the morning, stay still and don't move. Be aware of the first thought that pops in. Was it "Oh, no, another Tuesday!"? Or was it perhaps "This is going to be a wonderful day!" Set a daily intention. For example, "I intend to be peaceful, happy, and humorous today." "I intend to attract my perfect partner today." "I intend to have a loving and fun visit with my dad today."

Take a few deep abdominal breaths, close your eyes, and invite the divine in. Visualize the pure white light of unconditional love resting at the top of your head. Feel the warmth of the divine's hands on your head. Allow this white light to penetrate down into your whole body. Hold the intention that this white light is cleansing you of any unwanted or unhealthy beliefs or thought forms; feel the light penetrating into your cellular level, releasing old memories and beliefs that don't serve you. Keep breathing. Say, "I am now connecting with the universal consciousness and breathing in the highest vibration of peace and love." Ask the divine, "How can I serve you today?" Listen quietly.

Thank the divine for orchestrating the many details of your day. Say silently, "I am in the perfect flow for my highest purpose." Visualize the white light around any business situation or event that you want to bless. Ask for and imagine the highest vibration of love to fill the inside of your room, and the hearts of all the people you are involved with today, as well as all family members and friends. Say, "I am now breathing in the purest air; my body is now energized and eager to operate for me at its fullest capacity. I appreciate all the green traffic lights that help me get to work on time, as well as the great parking space." Thank the divine that all your tasks are getting completed on time. Expected phone calls with new opportunities are happening on time; your business deals are closing easily; new customers or clients are calling. Say silently, "I am vibrantly excited for today and filled with inspiration. I'm tapping into the creative flow of new ideas and projects that are pouring into me. Wherever I go, everyone is welcoming me with smiling eyes and a warm glow. I have so much compassion, respect, appreciation, and love for all my coworkers, partners, business associates, clients, bosses, family, and friends. I am grateful for the quiet time in my day to reflect, breathe, and renew my energy, as well as to feel connected with you, the divine, and with my purpose. I love sharing my gifts with people, and others appreciate them as well. I feel comfortable, secure, and confident in all that I do today. My family is joyful and healthy today. I appreciate the nutrients from all the healthy food I will put into my body today. My body appreciates the movement and exercise I will give it today. Thank you for all the love I am sharing and feeling today. Thank you for the remembrance and knowledge of my life purpose and my wholeness. Thank you for helping me with loving thoughts today. I love today. I feel today. I love all beings including myself today. Thank you for this balanced, beautiful day. May all beings be at peace. I love you, universe."

If you want to lose weight and you're not happy with the way your tummy looks, begin by noticing your thoughts about your body. Do you tell your body how unhappy you are with it? Do you feel that your belly is ugly? If you intend to lose weight, begin by sending positive thoughts to your body. Tell your tummy how much you love it. That part of you contains emotions that have been there to protect you. Visualize the unwanted emotions releasing. Appreciate that they were there to protect you in some way, but let them know you don't need their protection any longer. Give them permission to leave. Each day send thoughts of love. Visualize the emotions melting away. Imagine the fat dissolving. See your tummy flat and toned, with a narrow waist. Set the intention that your belly is getting smaller every day. You can do this exercise for any part of your body.

Before doing the exercise below, clear away any unwanted beliefs that may hold you back from manifesting your desires. When we are completely clear about our desires, beliefs, and feelings, the universe has something to go on and can manifest what we request.

A simple illustration of this might be a man going into a restaurant and telling the person behind the counter that he'll have a ham sandwich—no, make that turkey—no, wait, make it chicken salad. Because this man is unclear on his desire, the universe pauses, and he is hindered from getting his lunch. Where in your life have you hampered or delayed your own manifestation because you were unclear about what you wanted? At the same time, divine timing is an important factor here, so don't get discouraged if you do all your work on your beliefs and intentions and yet you still haven't received what you want; trust that the divine always has a bigger plan than you can imagine for yourself at any particular time.

The objective is to create a story of how you want your life be in all areas. Write out your intentions. Put pencil to paper. Use creative imagery to visualize the best-case scenario. This will help you be clear, with a sharp focus on what you desire. Cover any and all areas in your life: romance, personal development, finance, body care, spiritual development, career, rest and relaxation, hobbies, physical surroundings, relationships. Allow yourself to imagine a life filled with everything you could possibly want, and especially with how you want to feel.

- Write this in the present tense, as if it were already happening.
- Include words you will hear people say to you, such as "I'm so happy you're in my life" and describe the feeling of accomplishment.
- See yourself in this situation you're creating, imagine it in color.
- Know that you can modify, update, and change your story at any time. This is your life creation.
- Positively anticipate receiving your creation.

Here are some helpful ideas to include in your story:

- What emotions fill your heart?
- Who is in your life?
- Who is in your home?
- Whom do you love?
- How are you contributing in people's lives?
- How many hours a week do you do this?
- What do you want to improve on in your spiritual development?
- Where do you do this and with whom?
- Do you have a market niche?
- How much income do you want?
- How do you contribute to world peace?

In addition to writing your story, purchase a small toy imitation or model of what you desire. Hold the object in your hand as your focal point, and infuse it with your energy. Just imagine that you're sending your energy into the object. If it's a new car, buy a small matchbox car of the color and make you desire. Write how it feels to drive this car, to look at the car. What does the new car smell like? Where are you driving it? Who is in the car with you? What does the car sound like? If it's a house you desire, purchase a small toy house in the color and style you want. If it's a dog, get a small toy stuffed animal of the breed you desire. If it's a new career, get something that symbolizes what you want to do or where you want to work. Follow all the steps above to finish your story.

If you desire a romantic partner, write a love letter to yourself. Give this love to yourself. You are writing this letter from you to you. You are telling yourself how much you love, admire, and appreciate you. Write it with all your senses. Write what you are feeling, hearing, smelling, touching. Create your own special jar or box for this love letter. Have fun decorating it, and hold the intention that you are putting your energy into the jar or box. Fold this piece of paper up and place it inside the special jar or box, close it or seal it off, and place it on your sacred altar. Send white and gold light around it and bless it. Always include "the divine's will be done."

Supportive Habits During Creation

While you are expanding your creativity, opening to more parts of yourself, exploring new territory, you may be in a vulnerable state, so surround yourself with supportive habits and like-minded people. Positive support in your life is tremendously empowering, especially when you are embarking on new experiences. If you don't have supportive people in your life, try other avenues: seek out an intuitive counselor, life coach, mastermind group, support groups, or networking groups that can hold sacred space for you on your life journey.

Read your intentions out loud and allow yourself to feel your enthusiasm. You may want to place your written intentions in your private intention jar or box. Bless them as you are placing them inside your jar and, perhaps, on your sacred altar. Picture white light around the jar or box. Have faith that whatever is meant to happen is for your higher good, and trust. If you feel out of balance, tired, stressed out, or frustrated, this is a good time to evaluate how you're spending your energy. You may be trying too hard, forcing things to happen. Back off, take a break, and allow room for the universe to help you. A healthy flow is one that will feel good. Don't get discouraged if your desires are not achieved in your time frame.

Seeing the World through the Eyes of Abundance

There is unlimited peace, unlimited love, unlimited joy, and unlimited gratitude. I cringe when I hear people speak of others in their line of business as "competitors." If we begin to see them as allies, we believe in the abundance the universe has to offer, which helps everyone. When we view someone else as our nemesis or competitor, we are falling into the belief system of "lack," which means we feel there isn't enough for everyone, and ultimately this hurts us. When we were really little, we were taught to help each other out through cooperation and teamwork. The focus wasn't on winning; we were taught to have compassion for our friends and others. Why not adopt the same philosophy—that there is abundance for all and that everyone is a winner. Can we really enjoy our winnings when we are sending bad wishes to the opposition?

By the law of attraction, sending good thoughts to our new allies will only increase and draw more abundance to us. Through my own observations, I see things slowly changing out there in the world.

Different places of business are supporting each other by promoting each other's endeavors, helping bring more business to each other. This creates a really nice energy for the customers to know that the businesses are supportive of one another. If you work in a business, think about how your customers will feel when you teach them they can buy from both companies. Change the whole dynamic of fierce competition to one of friends and allies. Call all your competitors today and ask how you can support one another. How can we create together? How can we serve together for the best and highest good of our clients? It's time we came together and faced the fact that we are all connected to one source, the creator of all there is.

Truth

Our hearts and spirits touch when we are telling the truth. When we are truthful we touch people on deep levels, connecting with the energy even more than with the words. We can sense when people are not being sincere with us. When we do, it doesn't even matter what they are talking about, because we are focused on their energy, body language, voice, and tone. We trust that what we're sensing is more accurate than the words.

I have found that people are very supportive when we speak the truth, much more so than when we try to hide things or pretend something other than our truth. Think of how you felt when someone's words or gestures didn't seem genuine, as opposed to when someone was being honest with you even though they felt vulnerable. When we are sincere with ourselves, we can be genuine and sincere with others. When we are not telling the truth, there is something inside us that we are not comfortable with. When we accept who we are in every moment, we are in our power. We don't need to put on airs or pretend we are someone else. Next time you are about to speak in a way that isn't necessarily your complete truth, ask yourself what it is about this subject that you are uncomfortable with. What are you hiding, and why? It's never about the other person. Don't let anyone hold you back from expressing your truth. Don't be afraid of anyone. When you are afraid to speak your truth to someone, you are giving your power away to that person.

Perceptions

In life we choose how we perceive and react to every situation. We always have a choice in how we interpret any particular situation. We can choose to understand an event in a way that uplifts and affirms us or in a way that robs us of belief and trust in ourselves. How we interpret a situation is based on our own life experiences, our personalities, and our level of growth. We can choose to have a positive or negative response. We choose our attitudes toward all external events in our lives.

I once had a client, who I will call Ted, who had a very challenging upbringing. He had a father who spent time in jail for living the life of a criminal, and a mom who was extremely strict and brought him to another country to live. She then married his father's cousin. He came to me at age thirty-four, requesting help breathing. He said he had energy stuck in his throat and had had stomach problems for most of his life. After his first session, he said he was able to feel energy moving through his body. I knew I had to find out how he perceived his life. I could sense such a sweet spirit within him. He knew he needed help, and because of his commitment to his son, he was determined to change to a healthier lifestyle, to be well. I worked with him on yoga breathing exercises and empowerment techniques. My intent for Ted was to help him feel more grounded and connected to himself and to help him identify how his life had gifted him with who he is today, so that he could perceive his upbringing in a different light.

If we perceive someone as rude, we will see them as acting in a rude manner. Once we shift our perception of this person to a higher vibration, changing what we focus on, the person will shift toward us. If we focus on seeing this person with eyes of compassion and love, we will see another side to them. I have done this with people, and it works because what we choose to focus on, is what we will draw to us through the law of attraction.

Often we cling to old perceptions of who we once were, even though now, years later, we are not the same person. Who we are today is not who we were five years ago. Because of our life experiences, we are wiser, stronger, smarter, and more confident, courageous, peaceful, and self-assured. We are more comfortable in our skin and more at peace with who we are as human beings. We have lived five years filled with tears of sadness and of joy, peace, confusion, disappointment, shame, guilt, excitement, happiness, jealousy, love, and fear. But we got through all those situations. Those situations brought us to who we are today. We will never be that other, earlier person again.

Read these scenarios through and notice how you would interpret and respond during situations that arise in your own life.

1) You enter your office in the morning, and your boss calls you in for a meeting. She informs you that one of your major clients was taken away from you and given to a new hire; therefore, your pay will be lowered. Your boss explains that it has nothing to do with your productivity or performance.
   a) You get angry with your boss and become belligerent, yelling and calling her names.
   b) You wonder what you did wrong, and feel like a victim while blaming others.
   c) You express your disappointment but accept the situation and understand that this is meant to be. You trust that this

will now allow more time for you to attract another client that will be a better fit.

2) You are cooking for a special dinner party. You noticed that the main course is a little overcooked, but you don't have time to prepare a new meal.
   a) You serve the meal anyway and know you will do better the next time.
   b) You're extremely angry through the entire dinner, but you serve your meal anyway and make your apologies to the guests.
   c) You cry and feel depressed, throw out the meal, and inform the guests that you will be picking up takeout.

3) Your best friend of many years informs you that he or she doesn't have to time talk to you every day, because she/he is very busy.
   a) You call your friend every day anyway.
   b) You feel hurt and tell your friend all the things you feel is wrong with him or her, and you take it personally, wondering what is wrong with you.
   c) You give your friend space and send blessings to him/her.

4) Driving home from work, you are aware that you're driving ten miles over the speed limit. You get pulled over. The police officer comes to your window and asks if you know how fast you were going.
   a) You inform the police officer that you were not speeding and that you plan to fight the ticket in court. You blame the police officer for giving you a ticket.
   b) You apologize to the officer and admit you were speeding. You understand that this is a good reminder to slow down. You also see this as a sign that obeying the law is important.
   c) You begin to cry or flirt, hoping to get pity from the officer.

5) You open your refrigerator and two opened yogurt containers spill out, making an awful mess.
   a) You smile, take a breath, and clean it up, deciding that it was meant to be because you have been putting off cleaning the refrigerator.
   b) You yell at someone else in your house for leaving the yogurt opened inside the refrigerator.
   c) You call yourself an idiot for rushing and knocking the containers over. You wonder to yourself, "Why does everything bad happen to me"?

6) Your boyfriend or girlfriend breaks up with you.
   a) You are angry and want revenge.
   b) You blame him or her for ruining your life.
   c) You allow yourself time to adjust to the change; you trust that this is for your best and highest good. You thank this person for sharing your life, for learning and growing with you. You bless him or her.

7) For the first time, your assistant, Bill, forgot to cancel an order, which ended up costing you money.
   a) You yell at him and fire him for being incompetent.
   b) You have compassion for Bill, knowing he hasn't made this mistake before. You have a constructive conversation with him, discussing solutions for the future.
   c) You dock Bill the money out of his paycheck and remain angry all day.

8) You are at your condominium pool with your puppy. Your neighbor, who is swimming in the pool, stops and yells at you to get your dog out of the pool area "right now!" She continues to yell, "Don't you see the sign that says 'No pets'?"

a) You look her in her eyes and tell her to put a sock in it.
b) You realize that you were not obeying the rules, and take responsibility by removing the puppy. You didn't like the woman's attitude toward you, but you decide to pray about it and release any anger you may have felt.
c) You take her remarks personally, feel offended, and go inside your condominium to call your friends and other neighbors and complain about how rude she was.

These questions are an opportunity to see how we perceive life, adjust, and react to things as they arise in the moment. By our responses, we can see what our thought processes are. When things go awry, the optimist views the world with a perception that there are new friends, new opportunities, new jobs, new ways to earn money, new lovers—focusing on what is possible. Do you tend to feel sorry for yourself and feel like a victim to someone or the world? Do you get angry and lash out? Do you take life as it comes, trusting that there's a reason for everything? Maybe we do a combination of these things from time to time, depending on the circumstance. The sooner we can let go, the sooner we are at peace.

Visualization

This is the visualization of a happy and successful outcome, and it can be done for any situation. Visualize a situation you want to create in your life. Place pure emerald light around the situation or people involved. Visualize yourself already doing or being whatever your desired outcome is. Visualize yourself feeling happy, peaceful, and smiling. Maybe you're laughing; if so, what are you laughing about? What are you wearing in this visualization? Who are you speaking to? What are you doing? Visualize yourself feeling confident while speaking. Imagine all the people involved listening with great interest to every word you have to say. Feel the energy exchange of the situation. Feel yourself surrounded by loving people. Visualize them shaking your hand and closing the deal, or responding back to you in a positive light. Allow yourself to feel what it would be like to have a thoroughly successful outcome. Create the most positive situation and outcome possible. Use your imagination and creativity. Send love, peace, and light around the entire visualization. Notice the essence of how you feel having these wishes already come true. Trust, have faith, expect your desired outcome, and let go of it.

Intention Exercise

I intend to draw peace into my heart.

I intend to live a consciously aware life filled with love, gratitude, and abundance.

I intend to imagine the best scenario in all areas of my life.

Prayer

I pray for the balance and harmony of the earth and all its oceans, lakes, land, deserts, mountains, rivers, and forests.

Please, divine, help me to change my perspective for my highest potential and the highest good of all.

Divine, please send love to all beings in the universe.

Joy Journal

Allow yourself time to doodle. Just get lost in the moment and allow your creative juices to flow.

Gratitude Journal

At the end of each day, write down every time you were able to bring yourself to a place of peace when your self-doubts and fears popped in. What did you do that helped you in that moment? What were your positive expressions today?

Affirmation

I am reliable and responsible.

I am a powerful creator.

I am honorable and truthful in all my relationships.

Request

1. Observe what is working in your life; write these things down at the end of each day. Notice how your beliefs in those areas are supporting you. How can you change your beliefs in the areas that are not working in your life?

2. Create a scrapbook poster of everything you desire in your life. Cut pictures and words out of the newspaper, old cards, and magazines.

Chapter 4
Finding Humor in Your Life

Humor comes from a temperament and attitude of not taking life so seriously and not taking yourself so seriously. We can have more fun when we aren't so concerned about what others might think, and when we are not personalizing situations. We laugh at our mistakes and allow ourselves and others a margin of error, thereby avoiding the relentless stress of trying to be perfect. While enjoying the ongoing comedy in life, we look for the silver lining in every situation.

It's fun to have imperfections. Everyone has them; it's how we learn and grow. The pressure of being "perfect" is a surefire way to take the joy out of life. A person stuck in a world where perfection is high on the priority list is caught up in a never-ending web of always trying to look and be a certain way and have things just so.

I had a client who came to me because he was having trouble sleeping. As we talked, I discovered he was a perfectionist; when he awoke in the middle of the night (which many of us unfortunately do), it was unacceptable to him. So he created anxiety, and because of his anxiety about waking up, he wasn't able to go back to sleep. He felt he was not in control; the desire to control everything is a trait of perfectionists. Through creative imagery sessions, I worked with him on changing his focus to joy—so much joy that it outweighed his worries about winning or achieving. I asked him if he was happy with his perfectionism, and he said no, that his ultimate goal was to relax and have more peace and joy. He now sleeps soundly at night, and if he wakes up, he knows he'll fall back asleep. He is also learning to use his own imagery in order not to care about what others think, to let himself just have fun by relaxing the pressure he exerts on himself.

To lighten up is to allow your imperfections to bring you joy! Allow yourself the honor of being enough just as you are for one moment, without trying to reach for the next step on the ladder. Tell yourself you are amazing, awesome, talented, right now. Laugh at yourself when you do silly things, and others will laugh with you. Each of us is here to grow into deeper levels of compassion, love, and joy. We can choose to live through our lessons in a humorous, lighthearted way or not. We choose the attitude for each occasion. It doesn't matter if we're famous and on TV, a millionaire, or a homeless person; we all will experience a variety of losses: ended relationships, financial loss, illness, death. These things are a part of life. Allowing our imperfections to be seen is part of being authentic and sincere; it's part of embracing all the parts of us, and it's actually freeing to know that our imperfections are just perfect.

Choose to see the joy and blessings in the lessons or challenges of life. Don't blame the circumstances and take on the role of victim. Find the humor in the situation, take a step back, and become an observer. Go with the current in a fluid manner; stay flexible. Since life is always changing, we are living mostly in moments of transition. Breathe, stay calm, and resist the urge to control or manipulate. This makes it easier to get through these transitions. Choose to see the positive side of every situation. That doesn't mean you won't have moments when you feel overwhelmed, but you can still have an attitude that everything happens for a reason. Seeing life this way keeps us open to seeing new possibilities and keeps our energy open to receiving them.

Let's say you have a really great customer who is paying you a lot of money, but this customer isn't reliable. One day you get an e-mail from him telling you that he isn't interested in your services anymore. If you truly believe that everything happens for a reason, you will know down to the core of your being that new customers will flow into your life. You believe in abundance; there are many customers for you. Allow this customer to leave, bless him, and thank the divine for the new customers that are entering your life.

How can we take life more lightly?
- Remember to take deep belly breaths.
- See the good in people and everything.
- Find the humor.
- Appreciate big and little things.
- Be immersed in the present.
- Stay open to new ways of doing things, or new ideas.
- Be patient.
- Trust in your dreams.

A client of mine was under the impression that in order to be successful she had to push herself every day and work really hard, and be very serious. This attitude cost her in her relationships with female coworkers, because she didn't allow herself to relax and enjoy her time during her workday. She held on to a belief that if she were to relax and enjoy herself, that would be lazy. Laziness was a very negative attribute to my client; therefore, she made sure she was never lazy, and kept pushing herself. My client was already making six figures and was very successful. I asked her if she felt she was successful; I asked her what she was running to. Something clicked, and she changed her beliefs and decided to have more fun in her life by taking herself a little more lightly. To help deepen this intention, I suggested she mend fences with coworkers and create a homey feeling in her work environment with plants, pictures, and a comfortable wicker chair.

The truth is, everything is always in divine order. I believe that before we were born we were in the spirit world with our angels and all the divine beings that surround us, and we were given a blueprint for our life, which contained important lessons, our major life purpose, our love interests, and the knowledge that we are eternal. So if we were put here in this life to learn about self-love and empowerment, we may have situations in life to challenge us in this area. You've heard the saying "God doesn't give us anything we can't handle"? I'm sure that at times we may feel a bit challenged or confused by our life situations, but with perseverance, we always get ourselves out of it.

Funny Life Experiences

After getting enough yoga teacher training hours behind me to begin teaching yoga, I made my first yoga teaching call to a health club and made an appointment with the director of the fitness programs. She generously agreed to meet with me since she was interviewing for a new yoga instructor. She liked my enthusiasm, thank God, because at that point I didn't have a day of teaching experience behind me. She told me I could come on a Sunday and teach a trial class. I was so excited! During the class, which the director attended (to my great unease), I put the heat on to warm and protect everyone's joints and muscles, and then I lit a candle, when the director suddenly told me to put it out and that the room was too warm. Then, as the class continued, I asked everyone to go to the mirror for what I considered to be a great quad exercise, and immediately the director warned me that no one was allowed to touch the mirror. Then there was the stereo system, which I couldn't manage to get to work properly, and of course, as I was lighting incense, you-know-who put a stop to it. This all happened in a single one-hour class! When I called the director a week later and asked what she'd thought of the class, she replied, "I don't think it's a good fit." I chuckle every time I think back on this experience. We've all had these experiences when starting something new. Life provides great comedic material to enjoy.

Observe yourself in these sorts of situations and notice how you react. Do you remain calm and respond with humor and lightheartedness, or do you get upset and express anger or frustration? How do our decisions in those moments of choice affect others and ourselves?

Here's another odd thing that happened some time ago. I was on the phone with a coaching client, guiding him through breathing exercises to help him have better focus and alertness. This was only my second session with him, so we didn't know each other well. He was at home sitting in his La-Z-Boy chair and doing rapid breathing through his nose. The technique was new to him, as were some other meditation exercises I'd given him, but he was open and being a great sport about it all. As I was listening to him breathe, it suddenly struck me how funny it was to have this grown man breathing loud and fast on the phone. I started chuckling and had to hit the mute button twice. Then he said to me in a joking voice, "If my wife walked in now, she'd wonder what I was doing!" I undid the mute feature and started laughing out loud as I pictured the scene, and I told him I'd had him on mute twice because I couldn't control my laughter. He then asked me where the Candid Camera device was, and seemed sure this was a hoax and that he was being taped for TV. He said he always knew he'd end up on Candid Camera, and actually began looking around his room for the hidden eye. We laughed together, and I felt a special bond with my client. He said he would continue the breathing exercises but would probably have to do them in his car, where nobody could surprise him. It was a funny moment.

Two months after my mom was diagnosed with pancreatic cancer, my family had to pack up the only home we had known our entire lives—for over thirty years—because my dad was moving my mom to Florida. I must say, this was the saddest time in our family. We were all in a daze, our hearts in such sorrow and pain, all of us coping in our own way. I was hanging on to an imaginary rope connected to spirit. My dad, my older brother, and two of my friends were all helping with the last-minute walk-through of the family house, and we were grabbing anything left behind by the movers. There was a huge oil painting, about ten by twelve feet, on the wall, which had been accidentally overlooked (or maybe it wasn't an accident. My mom hated that painting!) My dad asked one of my friends and me to carry this huge painting down the street and give it back to the artist who painted it (or at least that's what I thought he wanted me to do). So with my longtime friend Mary Ann, I headed down the road, a half mile from my parents' house. We were cracking up as we pictured how funny we must have looked to the cars driving past us. When we got the painting up to the front door, I rang the bell, but no one answered. We decided to position the painting carefully up against the door and place something against its bottom so it wouldn't fall over. We were pleased with how we had secured the huge painting, and when we retraced our steps the half mile back home, my dad was out in the driveway watching us as we walked up to the house. I was proud of our accomplishment, but my dad was looking at me with a confused look on his face.

He asked, "Where were you?"

That's a silly question, I thought, since he's asked us to return the painting. I replied, "What are you talking about? We just got back from returning the painting, like you asked."

He looked at me, grinning, and said the neighbors had moved about ten years ago; it should have gone to the Silvermans in the opposite direction.

My friend and I were laughing uproariously as we thought about carrying the painting all that way to the wrong house, and thinking what a surprise it would be for the people living there when they saw a big (and not entirely attractive) painting looming at their front door. We still laugh about it today.

Play Exercises for Instant Joy

Being playful is an important aspect of expressing our natural essence. A playful frame of mind is the ideal emotional state for tapping into creativity, inspiration, and intuition. This attitude helps you stay open to thinking outside the box and reaching beyond the obvious. You will be open to possibilities in your life as well as have a high-energy vibration. The divine wants us to have fun, laugh, giggle, and enjoy life as much as possible.

Notice how many of these thing you already do, and how regularly. See if you can have fun doing most of the things on this list within the next month, and feel free to add your own things to the list.

- Sing to yourself.
- Doodle and allow your mind to wander.
- Dance around your house to your favorite song.
- Laugh at yourself.
- Kiss a loved one.
- Read a funny book.
- Run through your house naked like a kid.
- Write your own song and sing it.

- Play a fun board game
- Go on a picnic.
- Play with a baby.
- Buy a new ethnic cookbook and make a grand dinner.
- Drive a different way home and explore the new sights.
- Play with your pets.
- Listen to a tape of people laughing.
- Draw pictures of your most joyous moments.
- Play games outdoors.
- Drive through a fast-food restaurant and pay for the order of the car behind you.
- Make something artistic for someone else.
- Make yourself a special cake with candles, even if it's not your birthday.
- Do cartwheels on the beach.
- Skip outside around your house.
- Chew your food with your mouth open, like a child, enjoying every bite.
- Give your partner a fun fashion show of all your favorite outfits.

Spread your joy into the world every day of your life! Smile at people; acknowledge people everywhere you go. Try this all day long and you will be amazed at the joy you receive and give to others. Just by doing that, you are making a huge difference in the world. Don't you appreciate it when a stranger speaks to you in a store? Live consciously and notice things around you; appreciate everything and spread your love, light, and joy. Share your joy with others. Acts of kindness increase serotonin levels in the body and stimulate and strengthen your immune system; they also decrease depression.

The list below is made up of moments of kindness—things that happen all the time. These are the things we must focus on and not take for granted. The more we appreciate these things, the more lightly we can live life. Read each of the following items slowly, and breathe in the feelings that each elicits inside you.

- Someone unexpectedly opens a door for you.
- Your neighbor brings your garbage can or recycling bin up to your garage.
- A stranger smiles at you.
- You notice that someone has walked by your car and put a couple of quarters in your expired parking meter.
- You call a friend on the phone and they answer saying, "I always have time for you."
- A stranger stops to help you with your car trouble.
- The car in front of you pays your toll.
- A friend shows up at your front door and brings you coffee.
- You didn't notice that the traffic light turned green, and instead of honking, the driver behind you waits patiently for you to notice on your own.
- You got lost driving around, and someone takes the time to lead you to where you need to be.
- A store owner lends you money because you left your purse at home.
- Your neighbor offers to walk your dog.
- A friend sends you a message to let you know how much they appreciate you.
- A family member calls you to let you know they forgive you.
- Someone offers you a ride to the airport.
- A friend shows up to support you during an important event.
- Your lawyer decides not to charge you for a visit.
- That special person in your life says, "I love you."
- Someone tells you how inspiring you are to them.

Living in the Moment

Living in the moment is just that: being present with all our senses as well as our thoughts. We are not thinking about what we need to get done for the future, and we aren't thinking about the past. We aren't concerned with anything but being immersed in the actual moment we're in. We can't be joyful if we are constantly living our pains of the past or worrying about chasing the future, because we are too focused on what could happen.

When we are truly living in the moment, we are not worried or anxious about anything. Why would we be? It's a waste of time to put a lot of attention on what we think we should or could have done in the past. It's a waste of time to focus on what we don't have in our lives. It takes us out of the present to focus on something that is already done and can't be changed. This way of being is known as living in the past. You can't go back and change it. You can learn from it and move forward. We don't have to think about how to get to the future; it will happen on its own. We set our goals and intentions, trust and let them go, and move in the direction of our desired outcome. And we aren't attached to the outcome, either. If things don't occur to our exact specifications, we stay open to a bigger plan. While we are living life, we are focused on the task at hand, breathing, believing, loving, and appreciating—giving our attention fully to everything in every moment.

Full engagement is an opportunity to be completely focused and immersed in the present by managing your energy. Professional athletes understand this kind of focus. In the book *The Power of Full Engagement*, Jim Loehr and Tony Schwartz state, "Performance, health, and happiness are grounded in the skillful management of energy." Embrace your life now. Every person you come into contact with deserves your full attention, as does everything you do, including rest. Resting is an opportunity for you to renew your energy. Allow yourself time to rest your mind and body. According to *The Power of Full Engagement*, it's important to "switch the channel" every 90 to 120 minutes. Allow your energy and brain to renew themselves by taking short breaks throughout your day; take a walk or a bike ride, meditate, pray, breathe deeply, talk on the phone, chat with friends or coworkers, read a book or magazine, sit outside, take a shower, play with a child, do yoga stretches, write in your journal, listen to music—whatever allows your brain an opportunity to relax. This has really helped a coaching client of mine. He said he customarily took such breaks, though he viewed them as instances of "procrastination," but now he allows himself these healthy breaks without the guilt, because he understands their importance and sees the benefits of being more focused and energized throughout his day.

Make everything an act of love, and discover the gift in every moment of your life. Next time you do the dishes; try to stay focused on every minute detail about washing the dishes. If your mind wanders, thank it and bring your attention back to the task. Feel the water on your hands. Smell the dish soap. Let yourself be absorbed in the whole process. Be fully engaged. It will allow a higher concentration of energy to be focused on whatever you are doing.

If we put conditions and huge expectations on ourselves and then beat ourselves up for not "getting there" soon enough, this is self-defeating behavior. After all, where is "there"? What are we chasing? Why don't we stop and accept ourselves right now, in this moment, and enjoy our journey? The journey doesn't end. We are always trying to get somewhere, always desiring something, and when we reach where we intended to be, we aren't even at peace—we're running to be somewhere else. The journey is more important than the destination. Have patience with yourself; live one day at a time. Have you ever enjoyed being where you are? Why do we think we will be better or happier when we have this degree or that certification, or get married, move to a new city, get a raise, have a new house or car or more friends? This is attaching feelings to things and people. Love, embrace, and accept yourself now. We have only this moment. So take a deep breath and realize that there is nothing to chase, nowhere to go. Enjoy the journey; revel in the process of life.

Integration of Feminine and Masculine Energy

Every person has feminine and masculine energy; it's the *yin* and *yang*, which are inside all of us. The key is to feel the balance of the two sides and know when to harness more of your masculine energy and when to use more of your feminine energy. Feminine power is associated with inner strength, softness, wisdom, intuition, creativity, nurture, compassion, receptivity, and self-assurance. Feminine power is not coming from ego, jealousy, insecurity, and fear—just the opposite. You know you have reached that place of feminine power when conflicts arise and you observe your reaction, attitude, and feelings inside first before responding and acting. You confront conflict without the need to prove that you know more than someone else, or prove that you are the one in charge, or that you're smarter, or retaliate out of anger, or try to make another person feel inadequate. True feminine power is "statement energy"—you state the facts in confidence and assurance and are detached from what others may think.

The left side of the body is considered the feminine side; the right side, the masculine side. The right hemisphere of the brain corresponds with the left side of the body, and the left hemisphere corresponds to the right side of the body. You may have heard that right-brain people tend to be creative, intuitive, artsy, easy-going, type B personalities. And you have probably heard that left-brain people are type A personalities: analytical, driven, fast-paced. But the truth is, both sides, feminine and masculine, must feel equally important and must be allowed to become integrated as friends.

Masculine energy is analytical and logical and is associated with action, aggression, muscular energy, control, will, ego. In my earlier days in corporate America, I thought power and strength came from being aggressive. I had an imbalance of yin and yang—I was expressing yang. A person with strong feminine energy may have a hard time taking action and getting things done. On the other hand, a person with strong masculine energy may be controlling and impatient.

Use this visualization technique when you want to create more harmony with your male and female energy:

Have your masculine and feminine sides communicate and become friends. Choose a name for each of them and introduce them. Get a sense of how comfortable they feel with each other. Ask what they need from each other. You can see it as energy or colors. Tune in to how both sides feel to you and with each other. Tell each side that you value, love, and appreciate them equally. Let each one know how important they are in your life. Ask each side if they are comfortable expressing themselves, and listen to what they have to say to you. See the colors dancing together and integrating into you, balanced and harmonized.

When I first began my yoga practice, it was more yang related, known as "power yoga," using a great deal of muscular strength. Over the years, as I was creating harmony between my two sides, and moving more into my heart, my yoga practice became less muscular and more balanced. Once again, our external world is mirroring our internal world. It's an ongoing consciousness. It's not something that you think about once and it's handled for the rest of your life. I believe that a great deal of how we are programmed is learned from our childhood, and it can take some work over the long haul to change it.

The balance between our feminine and masculine energy changes as we go through life. For example, when a woman becomes a mom, she may have more feminine energy, nurturing her young. When a young man is beginning a family, he may be more motivated to be the provider for his family by being task and action oriented.

Balanced Energy in Corporate America

In the corporate world, a woman should maintain "statement energy." Statement energy is an energy of confidence, stating the facts without any other agenda, holding one's own energy while making statements or presenting one's findings and research. Feminine energy takes into account other people's feelings and respects each person as an individual. When people are really confident and grounded inside, they don't need to put down or mistreat anyone. They can allow their inner light to shine because they are not threatened or intimidated in any way. Such people can help others to shine without being jealous. Their presence automatically uplifts others just by virtue of their balanced, peaceful energy.

How to be balanced with "statement energy":
- Dress within the guidelines provided by your company: professional attire.
- Be who you are without the need to pretend to be someone else.
- Speak the facts; take responsibility without drama or blame.
- Speak with compassion.
- Speak in a tone and voice of self-assurance.
- Feel equally confident when speaking to men or women, ask questions, and do needed research.
- If you don't know an answer, don't fake it; say you'll find out.
- Be a good listener; allow others to finish thoughts.
- Allow your creativity to come forth; use brainstorming and thinking out of the box to find solutions.

- Keep your sex life private.
- Use your appropriate strength for a handshake. In business I could always tell when a woman would try to prove her power by her handshake. There's no need to squeeze someone's hand really hard, but at the same time you want to give a firm, sincere handshake. Engage your whole hand, not just your fingers.
- Maintain good eye contact.
- Stand up straight, shoulders back, head up, with ears over shoulders.
- Wear colors that you feel good in.
- Ask for what you want: promotion, raise, office, or anything else that's appropriate.

Exercise: Rehearse your twenty-second tagline of who you are and what you're selling or promoting. First rehearse by yourself, and then try it with family members and friends.

See yourself dressed in a suit. Using a firm handshake, say your name with confidence: "My name is_____, and I do this for a living:_____."

Now describe in three sentences what you do and what is unique about it.

Describe why you are good at what you do.

Power comes from knowing who you are and being comfortable and confident with yourself. When you are comfortable and confident inside, you don't feel the need to defend or protect yourself. You respectfully honor your boundaries and others' as well. And you can admit your weaknesses and show your vulnerability without any shame. Being vulnerable is opening to your own power and heart. There is something very powerful about expressing your vulnerability; it allows your heart to be exposed. It exposes your truth.

During my fifteen years in corporate America, I was in all different sizes of companies—small to large, private and public—in positions ranging from manager to vice president. I believe this book applies to how we can flourish in the business world as well as in the other aspects of our lives, allowing our hearts to be present by showing compassion and respect for employees, employers, and coworkers. If we can create an environment where everyone feels connected to the daily tasks, to the company's goals, and philosophy, and to its clients or customers, we have a winning formula. All the members must feel that they are affecting the bottom line. If we value our team, seeing the employees as the foundation of our service or product, then we can build a sturdy ship. If the foundation begins to crack, we will have problems: dissension, disorganization, and chaos. The company foundation must be built on respect, compassion, gratitude, support, kindness, intuition, acknowledgment, and intelligence. Each employee wants to feel valued more than anything else. It's important to make an investment to keep employees happy.

- Ask employees how their personal lives are.
- Have compassion whenever employees or coworkers are going through a rough time.
- Respect employees' time away from the office.
- Never deliberately embarrass anyone.
- Offer employee coaching.
- Develop appropriate time for training.
- Allow others to give their input.
- Give positive feedback regularly.
- Motivate positively, not with fear.
- Give employees annual raises and potential for growth.
- Include in the company handbook's general attitude expectations that everyone is to use "please" and "thank you"—no commands.
- Choose a charity for the company to donate to.

A client of mine wanted help in a relationship with a coworker. He said this woman was not very nice to him. My client felt that maybe his body language was offensive to the woman. He didn't know how to get his message across. I shared with him that I thought the energy between the two of them needed to change—this had gone on for over four years. I asked my client if he would be willing to pray to the divine for help with the relationship. He said he had never even thought of asking for help in such a situation; he had always thought he could handle it himself. It was an "Ah-ha!" moment for him. I asked him if he could take it a step further and send blessings to the coworker and actually visualize the two of them talking in a friendly, respectful manner. I suggested to him, during any disagreement, to watch his body language, to remain calm, take deep belly breaths, relax his face and jaw, not point fingers, not cross his arms or put his hands on his hips, and try to state his case using facts only. I suggested that in the heat of the moment, he stay away from using language such as "this happens so much" or "this isn't a difficult task—can't you get it right?"

Next I suggested that he express how their strained relationship affected him from a feeling standpoint—not to blame her for anything or analyze her behavior. Then I suggested that he express what he needs done, followed by a request. I suggested he then ask her how he can provide assistance or help her to achieve this. I also asked him how it would feel if he were to ask her to have lunch with him, to leave the work environment and take the opportunity to know each other better. He didn't feel comfortable with that idea—maybe after he prays about it there will be a shift in energy.

When confrontations occur over power, control, protection, fighting for your voice, jealousy, resentment, or whatever it might be, you have the opportunity to go deeper, to open your heart more to your employees, subordinates, bosses, and coworkers. These people are in your life as your "teachers" to teach you something about yourself.

During a disagreement, instead of arguing back, decide to change the energy because, as you know, like energy against like energy never solves anything. In order to change the energy to a higher vibration, the change must begin inside you. You must be able to get into an authentic loving space with this person without feeling the need to defend yourself. Once you are in this loving space, you can communicate your thoughts in a sincere manner. The corporate world offers blessed opportunities to find joy, to expand your heart. I, for one, have had many such opportunities. I didn't always pick the high road — it took many years of lessons to realize I don't need to defend, or prove anything.

I was in an argument many years ago with someone in my department at work. I went home and prayed for love to be sent her way, even though I was angry at her behavior. I put that anger aside and sent her love. I visualized it going from my heart to hers and surrounding her whole being. The next morning she walked into my office and, without a word, set a lovely potted plant down on my bookshelf. It was her way of saying she was sorry. I was pleasantly surprised. I accepted her gift with appreciation.

The challenge is to train our minds to look automatically for the good and godlike part of everyone. If you are in an argument or confrontation with someone, ask yourself how the divine would view the other person. It's easy to see the negative aspects, but I encourage you to take the challenge and become more of an instrument of peace for the universe. When you notice things you don't like in another person, instead of letting yourself spin in that energy, be aware and bless the person. Send out a prayer for that person to feel their own love and divinity inside themselves. Send them love rather than hate, anger, or other negative feelings. Don't focus on all the things that are wrong with that person. Don't talk about all the negative things with other people. It's okay to acknowledge what you're feeling and observing, but instead of adding to the negative energy, bless them and send them thoughts of encouragement.

Try to love people truly and unconditionally, without judgment, actually to see the light, beauty, and gifts in all people, even if they are not being kind or you are not resonating with them. This attitude will put you in touch with a comfortable place inside you, a place of wisdom, surrender, humility, and trust. It's not about being right.

The divine doesn't turn away from anyone, saying, "Oh, I'm really not resonating with that person now, so I'll just judge him or her for being different, call them names and ignore their pain!" The divine knows that everyone is in the right place for them at the time. Our true connectedness is revealed when we feel the pain of another or when we perform even the simplest act of love and kindness. You have perhaps had an experience when someone was so loving to you it actually helped you open your own heart. Unconditional love heals. If you want more love in your life, give love. If you want more joy, be joyful. If you want more friends, be a good friend and reach out to others. Think where in your life you can give more love.

Send love, blessings, and compassion to your coworkers, peers, and superiors. Have more patience and tolerance; give them room to grow in their own time. Love them even when they do not love themselves. Get to know people on a deeper level, and learn what's underneath their behavior. There is no need to protect your rights or voice through a power struggle with someone else; no one can hurt you unless you decide to be hurt. What a gift it is for you to expand your heart more, on a daily basis. Be secure enough in yourself and your belief in abundance.

Most of us spend more hours awake in our work environments than we do in our homes. It's important to create a harmonious working environment for yourself. Surround yourself with pictures of your loved ones and your pet, with plants, pictures with your favorite colors, inspirational sayings, maybe a nice rug or wicker chair, shells and sand from your favorite beach in a nice bowl, pictures of your favorite destination—sunsets, mountains, flowers, beaches, deserts—or of your favorite sport. Surround yourself with anything that makes your feel good that is allowed in your particular office setting. Keep your office space organized and clean so you can perform at your highest level.

Every human being is important to the whole universe; everyone is loved equally in the divine's eyes. No one is better or worse based on how much money they make, what color their skin is, what language they speak, or what name they have for the divine. I believe everyone has a divine purpose for being here and is part of the creation as a whole. We are all an essential part of the fabric of consciousness.

Visualization

Go to your sacred space in or outside your home. Sit comfortably or lie down, close your eyes, breathe. Relax all your muscles. Think back to a situation in your life, maybe one of your most embarrassing moments, and feel the laughter, joy, and humor in it. Breathe. Let yourself smile, then laugh. Feel this laughter throughout your whole body. Laugh out loud. See each organ and cell as smiling and then laughing.

Intention Exercise

Consider the following major areas of your life. Create a list of intentions for each category. For example, I intend to have a more intimate conversation with my best friend. I intend to have more business. I intend to draw perfect health to me.

- Relationships (family, friends, coworkers)
- Physical health
- Spiritual and personal development
- Career
- Finances

Prayer

I pray to see the humor in my life and take things more lightly;

I pray for miracles of love and compassion for America's adversaries.

I pray that all people have the courage and self-love to follow their hearts.

Joy Journal

Describe a situation in the past year that came unexpectedly. Write about the things you had to do (for example, be flexible, handle all the challenges it put before you). Describe the situation and how you reacted to it. What were you most proud of about yourself? How did your flexibility help your energy and that of others in the situation? How did you grow from the experience? It could be a minor event or something that was a turning point for you.

Gratitude Journal

Write about the gratitude you feel toward someone in your life. Describe how the love from this person encouraged you to open your heart more to yourself and to the world. Write about all the things that are working in your life and why you appreciate them.

Affirmation

I am pure joy, following my heart and trusting God.

I have a great sense of humor.

I am patient with my coworkers and peers.

Request

Bring to mind a family member, coworker, or friend who pushes your buttons and irritates you. Write a list of five positive qualities that person has, and really believe what you are writing. Read this list out loud every day for a week. Notice if there are any changes in the energy between you and the other person.

Chapter 5
Balancing Your Everyday Life

Instant joy comes from giving to others, making others happy and helping people. It is truly a gift and blessing to bring joy to others. Whenever we send out a loving, joyful thought, every time we share our passion and excitement, we are sending out a high vibration of love into the universe. Keep spreading your pure joy and love! In return, that same vibration goes back to you. When you're in a bad mood or sad or not having a good day, you can change your whole vibration and mood by doing something for someone else, even a perfect stranger. Just stay alert, and the opportunity will present itself. Placing your attention on helping others helps get you out of your own personal troubles, so that you feel better about yourself.

Another powerful way to help and give to others is by inspiring others to believe in themselves and their dreams. This can happen through the power of your belief in them, even when they don't have much belief themselves—see them already achieving their goal of getting good grades, excelling in their sport, getting the job of their desire, meeting their soul mate, getting married, living in their dream house, creating a prosperous company, receiving a promotion and raise, being healthy and fit. Whatever their goals are, see them as if they had already achieved them.

A memorable giving moment happened on a show that Oprah Winfrey aired in December 2003, highlighting a trip she and a group of some fifty people took to South Africa with the intention of giving presents and throwing parties for some underprivileged children living in there. She gave away 50,000 presents to children. Watching her television show, seeing the children cry tears of happiness, affected me on such a deep level that I had tears of joy pouring down my face! I was so touched and moved by the emotions, the joy, of everyone involved, I will never forget that show. Charity is a blessing to the whole universe. I felt connected to the whole process; it touched my spirit. There are so many wonderful organizations, charities, and foundations that already exist, it makes it really easy to participate in giving. Choose one that calls out to you, and have fun contributing.

There's a universal law of reciprocity, which seeks a balance between giving and receiving. Make sure you are being paid what you deserve for your services, and make sure you pay others adequately for their time and services. Notice whether you are comfortable with receiving. If you don't allow others to give to you, you are energetically cutting off abundance from flowing into your life. You must not only receive; you must do so in an attitude of appreciation, and you must feel worthy of receiving. Notice whether you feel that you give more than you receive financially or through the amount of love you give out. Are you charging enough for your services? Are you blocking money or love from entering your life? Do you give to others through altruistic acts or financially? Do you have an attitude of "the world owes me"? A healthy attitude is one of "How can I serve? How can I inspire others? How can I help?"

If we take advantage of people and don't pay for something adequately, it will affect us negatively. Trying to get a really good deal by taking advantage of someone creates disharmony in the balance of exchange.

Gratitude and Appreciation in Everyday Life

Gratitude is an expression of deep appreciation. This expression carries a very high vibration out into the universe. The universe is transformed with our gratitude. According to Dr. Masaru Emoto, author of *The Hidden Messages in Water,* being exposed to the words "love and gratitude" formed the most beautiful and delicate water crystal he had seen so far. Mr. Emoto goes on to say, "It was as if the water had rejoiced and celebrated by creating a flower in bloom."

Spend time appreciating even the small things we may take for granted, like the phone systems that allow us to communicate instantly all over the world; clean water to bathe in; the mail carriers who transport our letters throughout the world; the electrical appliances that wash our clothes and dishes; watches and clocks that keep time for us; our heating and cooling systems; traffic lights that control and make driving safe; the beautiful synchronicities of life. Sometimes we don't appreciate things until they aren't there anymore. Appreciate your body and overall well-being; the body has its own intelligence system and will respond to your love.

Focus on what you appreciate in your life. Begin to train your mind to focus on every little nuance that occurs during your day that is a positive experience for you, and say, "Thank you, divine." Share you appreciation and gratitude with other people who contribute to your life on a daily basis: the supermarket cashier, teachers, facilitators, doctors—everyone. Let people know how much you appreciate their time and energy. Just say "thank you." Your appreciation will uplift others. You are respecting and connecting with their spirit.

)wledge yourself with deep appreciation and gratitude for all your beautiful gifts, the special qualities you offer the world. Self-acknowledgment is more important than any compliment you can receive. Maybe you are a sweet, kind, and compassionate person because your parents modeled opposite qualities to you. There are always the polarities in life to learn from. Be thankful for those lessons, release your suffering, anger, blame, and shame, and find it in your heart to forgive. Write a list of how your parents, siblings, or others in your early life perhaps inadvertently helped you to become who you are today. Continue to focus on your beautiful qualities.

When someone gives you a compliment, take it into your heart and feel it. Acknowledge your appreciation for their kind words. We have all brushed off compliments for one reason or another, but try to feel them and allow them in. Why is it that we take in the negative comments from others so easily and yet brush away the positive ones? Practice this in your life. The giver of the compliment will be filled with joy by your appreciation, and you will feel better because your appreciation gave back to the giver.

At the end of each day, write your blessings in your journal with complete, heartfelt gratitude. Here are a few things to appreciate:

- Thank you for the peace and faith in my heart.
- Thank you for helping me with my thoughts, perceptions, and beliefs.
- Thank you for the daily miracles that occur and for my ability to recognize them.
- Thank you for caring for my family and friends.
- I thank you so much for helping me to discover my true passions and have the courage to move forward.

Enjoy every waking moment, whether you're washing dishes, driving your car, eating, cleaning the toilet, walking, writing, working, bathing your dog, or visiting a housebound senior citizen. When engaged in conversation with people, give them your full attention and show them how much you really care. Life is precious, and it's time to open our hearts and allow our light to shine brighter than ever to the world. The vibrational level on the planet rises every time we share our love and authenticity. According to Dr. David Hawkins, in his book *Power vs. Force,* "A few loving thoughts during our day can counterbalance all of our negative thoughts." Send blessings to everyone and everything.

Joy in Nature

Everything in nature has its divine purpose and place. The law of nature is one that exists in harmony and perfection. All nature is necessary for the harmonic order of creation. Trees, dry riverbeds, fish, flies, mountain lakes and mud holes, flowers and weeds, elephants and armadillos, oceans, snow, rain, rattlesnakes, and humans all exist interconnected, relying on the whole to sustain life. It's orchestrated as if by magic. In our daily lives we aren't even burdened with the creation of this glorious design, yet we are responsible for the continual harmony by respecting the system we live in.

Nature is the divine's exquisite tapestry, filled with colors, movement, energy, smells, sounds, and changing seasons—and it's free! How glorious and thoughtful of the divine to offer us this vast, ever-changing mosaic, this source of healing from the earth that is free and available to everyone. Look around and enjoy your surroundings. Appreciate Mother Earth, our gracious hostess, while we are here. We are the guests of this beautiful earth. We don't own it; we are just visitors here. Appreciate all the earth offers us, all the ways it supports us, feeds us, heals and sustains our lives. We must appreciate her as we would any other host. Write a heartfelt letter to the earth expressing your gratitude for hosting you during your stay here. Identify all the different parts of the earth you have visited, what you've enjoyed, what you have found beautiful, what landscapes you love the best, how much you love feeling the sun on your body, your favorite parts of nature. This letter will assist you in bonding and feeling the oneness between you and the earth.

Become one with nature. You may ask, "What does that mean?" It means to take in nature fully by drinking its vistas, smells, beauty, and life force into your body. Walk silently in nature and feel your connection with the earth's energy, which is very healing and grounding. Feel the earth beneath your feet. Lie down on the ground; feel the grass beneath you. Feel the sun penetrating into your skin. Place your hands on a tree or rock. Notice if you can feel an energy exchange. Hold the intention that you are absorbing the healing energy, the life energy, from the tree or rock, and in return send love back. Look at a flower with the intention of becoming one with it. Draw into you the scent of the flower; touch its leaves and smell your fingers; notice what the leaf and stem feel like; feel the petals; notice the softness and fragility of the petal. Feel this life force inside you; send love back to this flower. This life force is in everything.

Before disturbing anything in nature, ask permission from the earth, from the tree, from the rock, and get a sense whether it's okay. Be respectful and appreciative of nature.

My profession is to be always on the alert to find God in nature,
to know his lurking-places, to attend all the oratorios, the operas in nature.
—Henry David Thoreau—

Joy at Home

Create a joyous, nurturing home environment for yourself and your family. Place family pictures of fun outings or loving prayers on the walls; put your favorite candles on the tables; use your favorite colors on the walls. I had a woman come to my home and help me move furniture, plants, and pictures to create the optimum energy flow in my home, following the ancient Chinese principles of feng shui (pronounced "fung shway", literally, "wind-water"). It refers to the natural forces of the universe and is the ancient Chinese art of living in harmony with your environment and natural elements. It is the art of placement, proportion, and design, facilitating balance of energy in any given space while maintaining its free flow. It is used to determine the suitability and layout of homes, businesses, burial grounds, and temples to ensure optimal health, prosperity, and happiness.

Each room in a house has its own elements that should be in place, such as family and friend pictures on a particular wall for support in your life; awards, trophies, plants, and fish in a particular area; a mirror not facing a bed. The bedroom should be balanced with two lamps, two night tables, with proper positioning of the bed. Clutter and dirt should be removed. The result is a balance of energy, a feeling of openness. Look around your home and see if you can alter your own furniture to create an open feeling. If you're interested in learning more on this, get a book out of the library or contact a local feng shui specialist in your area.

Each color has its own vibrational frequency, which also ignites a powerful feeling inside us. We are attracted to the colors our bodies need. When choosing your colors for your home or to wear, let your intent be to choose shades that help heal and balance or that enhance whatever effect you desire. It's just as important to resonate with the color of your clothes as with their style. Buy your favorite flowers for your home, and enjoy their beauty and fragrance. Buy a blanket for your bedroom, in your favorite color and texture. Light natural scented candles and incense and fill your house with pleasing aromas. Cook tasty meals. Purchase a gemstone that has special meaning for you. Open all your windows and doors frequently, and cleanse the energy and invite in the fresh air and sunlight. Keep your house organized and clean. Listen to your favorite music; sound also can be very healing and help create specific moods. Read stimulating books and magazines. You can even buy or create a fountain in your yard or patio and listen to the calming, tranquil sounds of water. Colors, sounds, smells, and textures can change your whole mood. Give away everything in your life that doesn't bring you peace or joy; give away that old stuff that has been in storage for years. Throw out any pictures of yourself that you don't like; what's the purpose of holding on to them? Invite into your home like-minded people who support and encourage you. All these things that you choose to surround yourself with can raise your level of consciousness and create a harmonious, balanced home.

If you're interested in decreasing the amount of toxins you bring into your home, begin to purchase environmentally healthy cleaning products that can be purchased now in many grocery stores and most health food markets. Most cleaning products are not healthy for children, pets, or anyone. Use skin care products and makeup that are all natural. What we place on our skin penetrates into our bodies. Read labels and ask questions about the ingredients. You have the right to know what you are using and bringing into your home. Vinegar and hot water is a great cleaner for tile. For carpets, hot water without the chemicals works great. Use natural, organic, chemical-free products on your hair and face. Use testers and see what works for your skin and hair. There are many natural pesticides now that are not harmful to animals or humans.

Being in control of our external stimulation also means we can control what we watch on television. It can add to pollution in our homes. The media delivers information in a manner that can promote more fear, and this does not inspire us to live in love but instead only fuels the fear. It's important to stay informed, but just as we choose the books we read, music we play, conversations we engage in, people we associate with, and television programs we watch, so we can also select what we invite into our space out of the sensory barrage that passes for "news." We are choosing what types of vibration we are

bringing into our home environments. We can also choose to create
the energy of inspiration in our home for our families. The media is
not to blame; they are just giving the public what sells. There are more
inspirational stories than negative ones; there is more "good" in the
world than "bad"—we just don't hear about it as much. Our media is
already shifting because of our yearnings for deeper truth and meaning. There are more movies now that touch upon such themes as life
after death, spirituality, and angels. Once again, we wouldn't know
what an uplifting story is if we didn't know what a sad story is. The
polarities all exist together, but what do we saturate our lives with?
Choose to surround yourself with energy that feeds your spirit.

Listening and Connecting to Your Body

The body, spirit, and mind are connected, interrelated. The
health of the body is connected with the health of the mind. There
are many avenues to cleansing the body, but to sustain the health of
the body we must also look at the attitudes that affect our health. According to Dr. David Hawkins, "Physical and mental soundness are
attendant upon positive attitudes, whereas poor physical and mental
health are associated with such negative attitudes as resentment, jealousy, hostility, self-pity, fear, anxiety, and the like."

There are many cases that prove the mind-body connection. Dr.
Carl Simonton, author of *The Healing Journey,* created a cancer center
in California based on the concept that beliefs, feelings, and attitudes
are important factors affecting health. A major part of the healing
program is based on using meditation, visualization, psychotherapy,
prayer, and creative imagery to heal one's own body. Therapy is used
to help release pains from the past through forgiveness and to create
harmony with a newfound love. It's important to express communication and not let things build up. By expressing ourselves, we are
releasing stresses and emotions in a positive way.

We are a major part of our own healing process. If we have the desire to live, through our own will and a positive attitude we can send loving and appreciative thoughts to our bodies. In visualizations we can also communicate to our body parts and ask what they need from us to help them heal. We can learn to listen and trust what we hear. We can also use our imagination to bring healing energy and colors into our bodies to help repair and release stuck energy, emotions, or disease. If a person is not feeling well, it is prudent to imagine the body as being healthy, feeling healthy, and doing all the physical activity we want it to do. We are much more powerful than we give ourselves credit for.

In my early public-speaking days, I was on my way to give a talk to about ninety people, and I felt a bit nervous. Taking several deep breaths to relax, I imagined smelling lavender. Lavender is known to be very relaxing. With each inhalation I drew in the smell. As I smelled lavender I imagined I was sipping a cup of chamomile tea. Chamomile is known to be calming to the nervous system. I did this for a couple of minutes, and to my surprise, it worked—my jitters were gone. Use your imagination to create the best scenario for you.

Whatever is going on spiritually and emotionally can settle in the body. What a wonderful, immediate tool for us to work with! Listening to your body is a good way to "see" in this way. The body tells the truth of what is going on inside us with our emotions. Muscle testing, called behavior kinesiology, developed by Dr. John Diamond, is one way to test the body for answers. While you're holding one arm out to your side, a certified practitioner asks you questions while testing the resistance of your arm. If your arm is strong, with minimal movement, your body is responding "positive" to the questions, if your arm has significant movement, the response is "negative." Our muscles weaken with negative stimuli and hold strong with positive stimuli. Your body is responding correctly regardless of how you are verbally responding.

One of the most important factors in bodily health is breath. Breath helps remove energy blockages and stuck emotions in the body, mind, and heart and opens passages to allow optimum blood flow throughout the body, nourishing and cleansing it of imbalances and the buildup of toxins. This unhindered flow purifies the body, enhances healing, and prevents diseases from settling in the body. Deep, full breaths invite relaxation. And when the body is relaxed, we can calm the mind. Notice your breath, and if it tends to be shallow and confined to the upper chest area, bring it all the way down to your abdomen; if your exhalation is shorter than your inhalation, lengthen it for a balanced, full breath. Breath is the life force that connects us with spirit.

Proper body alignment is equally important. Be conscious of how you sit when you're in front of your computer or TV, in your car, or at the table. Straighten the spine, bring your shoulders back, shift your weight slightly back, stretch the top of your head toward the heavens, and line up your ears over your shoulders. With the aging process, many people begin to stick out their chin, so that it's often the first body part that enters a room. Most important, smile and breathe; frowning creates wrinkles! Correct body movement depends on proper alignment. Lying on your back over a large rubber ball is one way to align your spine; it allows stuck energy in your spine to move and flow. You may feel mucus clearing instantly from your throat. This is just one small thing you can do daily. Listen to your body, ask it what it needs from you, and respond. You may feel like doing a forward bend while standing, which allows the blood to flow toward your face and feels as if you were getting an internal facial. It also massages your spleen and liver, relieves stomachache, releases tension in your head, oxygenates the brain, and makes more energy available. You can do this forward-fold pose, called *uttanasana*, a couple of times a day. Most important, develop a relationship with your body—you know it better than anyone else. Tune in to it; move and stretch and give it what it needs, and don't forget love. Your body will respond with gratitude and health.

Balance

Balance of body, spirit, and mind is important to your inner peace. When energy is stuck inside the body and isn't flowing smoothly, divine intuition, creativity, and clarity can become blocked; it can also cause physical ailments and alter your mood. At the end of this chapter, you'll have the chance to complete a life balance worksheet that will help you get a picture of what and how often you engage in activities for your mind, body, and spirit. You can also use it to identify and plan activities in areas where you might benefit from being more engaged. Following are a few things you can do for your body, mind, and spirit.

Visualization Technique

Send love and appreciation to all body parts with this exercise. Take five minutes and do a complete body scan. Lie down and relax your body. Close your eyes and take several breaths in and out of your nose. Bring your attention to your toes. Notice how they feel. Send your love and appreciation to each part of your feet; silently thank them for working so hard for you. As you make your way up your calves, send your breath of love to your shins and knees. Thank them for working so hard for you every day. Continue throughout your entire body and each organ, checking in with how they feel. Ask each body part silently if it needs anything from you. Trust whatever you hear back. Maybe a part of your body needs rest, love, cleansing, exercise, massage, or touch. If you do find a sensation, you can place your hand gently over that area and imagine sending healing energy there. Ask the sensation what it needs from you. Notice if it represents a color or shape. Ask what this sensation represents to you. Do you need it any longer? Ask the color/shape if it's ready to be released. If so, see it draining down through your body and out the soles of your feet into the earth. Know that the earth will turn it into love. Now fill yourself up with white light. This is an opportunity for you to become more in tune with your own body, to give it the nurturing and love it requires. Your body will respond and be grateful for the appreciation and attention.

You can do the above exercise in the shower, too. Imagine the water as the divine's white light pouring onto your body, cleansing you and balancing your energy. As you're cleaning your body with soap and a washcloth, thank each part and send love to it; as you wash your hair, you are loving your hair, scalp, brain, eyes, mouth, ears, nose, and the largest organ of your body, your skin.

Listen intuitively to your body. Learn what foods agree or don't agree with you. Eat the things that agree with your digestive system. Notice what foods give you gas, indigestion, heartburn, diarrhea, constipation, headaches, a distended belly, stuffy nose. The foods that cause these symptoms are ones you want to avoid or, at the very least, eat sparingly; you may have a food allergy. You can tell what foods or meals agree with you when you don't have any of the symptoms listed above.

Notice if you have a balance between external stimulation and introspection time in your life. If your focus is extremely external, doing many physical activities, taking care of many people and in general being very social, notice whether you need more grounding and connection to spirit. Are you a good listener? It's imperative to have that balance of spirit connection, meditation, and quiet time to balance the physical activities. Notice what is working in your life and what isn't, and how you can make the necessary changes. I have also known people who spend most of their free time in meditation and don't enjoy physical activity.

Review this list of body, mind, and spirit activities.

Step 1. Write down the things you are already doing or are prepared to commit to.

Step 2. Write down "how often" you are committed to each activity.

Step 3. Periodically check in and see if you are maintaining a healthy balance.

Body

You can do any physical activity that includes walking, running, weight training, exercise classes, swimming, tennis, in-line skating, golf, rowing, massage, canoeing, yoga, Pilates, cross-training, aerobics, martial arts, or dance. Being connected with your body allows you to sense instinctively if something is out of balance. You become your own best doctor and caretaker. It's a good idea to cleanse the body of toxins periodically by eliminating sugar, caffeine, white breads, white rice, salt, meats, what products, and dairy. Speak to your doctor to choose an appropriate cleansing regime for you.

Mind

Find an activity that allows your mind to rest and your creativity to shine forth. Here are a few examples: reading, singing, music, games, puzzles, research, journaling, watching joyful, inspirational movies, writing, painting, vacationing, cooking, pottery, visiting with friends and family, designing clothes or furniture, building, sewing, breathing exercises, playing with babies, making a scrapbook, photography, studying any area of interest.

Spirit

Activities that nurture the spirit include meditation, visualization, energy work, sitting quietly, volunteering, chanting, being in nature, yoga, communicating with the divine, prayer, singing, sound therapy, touch therapy, listening to your own inner voice, playing an instrument, being in nature, and breath work.

Honor your needs and how you feel. If a part of your body feels stressed or in pain, or if you're coming down with a cold, just rest. Take a hot Epsom salts bath; do some diaphragmatic breathing; make sure you're drinking at least eight glasses of water a day.

Many alternative therapies are extremely beneficial for balance: body massage, chiropractic care, acupressure treatments, hypnotherapy, healing work with medical intuitives, Reiki healing, sound therapy, touch therapy, jin shin jyutsu, chi gong, rapid-eye therapy, energy healing, color therapy, and therapeutic touch. There are many others, and I encourage you to see what's available in your area and be open to new experiences. Try something new; see how you feel.

Fuel for the Body

Food, water, breathing, and loving thoughts are our best medicine. What we eat is the fuel our body runs on all day and night. It's important to take care of the inside and outside of our bodies. In the area of diet, from most of the information I've studied, as well as from my experiences with a nutritionist, the common suggestion is to eliminate or moderate consumption of the three whites—white flour, salt, and sugar—and limit intake of dairy products, saturated fats, coffee, and alcohol, while eating a great variety of greens, grains, and fruit. Each person's body makeup is different. There are many different philosophies that can be studied, but it's important that you follow a regimen that corresponds with how your body responds to various foods. I also agree with the philosophy of eating right for our blood type. Take responsibility for your own health and do research, get more than one opinion, read books, and follow your own guidance while listening to your body. I suggest going to a naturopathic, homeopathic, herbal, Ayurvedic, or nutritional practitioner as well as your medical doctor. Read labels and try to buy organic foods, so that you're not eating the pesticides, hormones, and chemicals otherwise contained in food. When you eat right, you will feel and look healthier. Eat slowly and mindfully, and enjoy every bite. Research shows that we control much of our aging process. Frequent, smaller meals speed up your metabolism and assist with sustaining even energy flow throughout the day. And try not to skip breakfast; it gives you the energy needed to give your brain a kick start. Drink lots of water, and, as always, belly breathe. When I don't feel well, I use natural remedies and have had good success. I have found it unnecessary to use antibiotics (or give them to my dogs) for many years.

Eat your food mindfully, appreciating every bite. Be aware of how the food feels inside your mouth. Is it crunchy, smooth, slippery, chewy, hot, cold, room temperature, sweet, spicy, bitter, mild, sour, tart, refreshing? What is your favorite food texture? Do you like hot, warm, or cold foods? In between bites, set your utensils down and take a deep belly breath. Really chew your food and allow your own saliva to wash the food down.

Visualization

Go to your sacred space in or outside your home. Sit comfortably or lie down, close your eyes, breathe, and relax all your muscles. Sit in your most natural, comfortable seated position with your spine straight, shoulders back, top of your head reaching to the heavens, ears in line with your shoulders. Close your eyes; connect with your breath, breathing through your nose. Bring the breath all the way down to your abdomen; notice how the breath feels coming in and out of your nose. Sit quietly for a minute, breathing in and out as you relax your whole body and calm your mind.

Imagine walking up a hill covered with a field of beautiful flowers among the tall grass, with all your favorite colors and scents. Feel the warmth of the sun on your face. Smell all the scents. Feel the grass under your feet. At the top of the hill is your enlightened self.

It's you as an enlightened being, looking down on you. As you reach the top of the hill, your enlightened self takes you in his or her arms and gives you a big hug. You both lie down on the grass together and look up at the sky. He or she says to you, "Ask me anything you want to know, and I will tell you from my perspective what I think." Silently ask your questions, and listen to the responses.

Notice what your enlightened self feels like. Remember the messages you were given. Ask for guidance in any situation, conflict, or relationship. Ask your enlightened self what she or he would do in a particular situation. Breathe and listen. When you're complete, thank yourself. Hug him or her good-bye and walk back down the hill to where you began. Remember how you felt around your enlightened self. What did you learn? Write down any important message or guidance.

Intention Exercise
  I intend to spend more time in nature.
  I intend to feel the connection between my body, spirit, and mind.
  I intend to live in a peaceful home environment.

Prayer
  I pray, dear Lord, that all beings who are suffering are healed in body, spirit, and mind and find joy in their everyday lives.
  I pray, dear God, that everyone feels grateful for life's everyday joyous moments.
  Please bless my family to resolve conflict and find common ground so they can better appreciate one another.

Joy Journal
Write about what inspires you, what motivates you each day. Make a "joy list," describing what brought you 1) more joy today, 2) this week, 3) this month. Write all the kind thoughts you have for yourself.

Gratitude Journal

Make a list of all the people you are grateful for in your life, and why. These can be family members, friends, acquaintances, living or dead, as well as people who may have touched your life in some way even though you didn't know them personally or maybe only knew them for a few minutes.

Affirmation

I am grateful for my carefree attitude.

I am balanced emotionally, spiritually, and physically.

I am blessed to feel joy in many of my life situations.

Request

1. Write letters of appreciation to people who have made a positive difference in your life, such as authors of books you have enjoyed, or a teacher, and let them know how important they are to you.

2. Have a "self-care" day. Do five things for yourself: dress up, treat yourself to a special meal, get a massage, take a nap, have a long, hot bath, buy yourself some flowers, take a short trip, curl up with a good book, go for a walk, spend time with your best friend, a grandparent, or someone else. Then do an act of kindness. Maybe clear out some of your old clothes or shoes and donate them to a charity, or show up at a friend's house and wash their car or clean their house.

3. Spend time outside in nature, planting herbs or flowers. Enjoy watering them, sending love to them, smelling them, and possibly tasting them.

The following worksheet will give you a picture of the things you do for your mind, body, and spirit. List actions under each heading (for example: hiking, biking, swimming, reading, lectures, cards, meditation, chanting, retreats), and see if you're concentrating in just one or two areas when you might benefit holistically from a more evenly balanced picture.

Life Balance Worksheet

Activities

Body: Times per week/month
1.
2.
3.
4.
5.

Mind:
1.
2.
3.
4.
5.

Spirit:
1.
2.
3.
4.
5.

Chapter 6
Relaxing with Your Heart

There is so much more going on in life than we even realize—a much bigger picture in the meaning behind specific situations and why they occur. At times we get too caught up in the little things in life. The bigger picture is how we affect one another; how we actually heal from certain situations; how we trust ourselves and follow guidance; how the universe uses us to help humanity; how we expand into our hearts, becoming wiser, more compassionate, more conscious.

In getting caught up in our own feelings and emotions because we are attached to outcomes, we don't see above our own junk to see how we benefit from situations. Here's an example. I was asked to give a talk to eighty-six women at a social luncheon. When I was told to keep it light and funny with some exercises, I asked my contact if she had a backup speaker, because my talks aren't really "light." She said, "Oh, you'll be fine; they'll love you—just don't do any partner exercises."

I was preparing for my pitch with a few main points, a funny story about my mom, breathing exercises, a forgiveness exercise, and a couple of other things. I expected the group to laugh a lot, love my talk, and hoping for referrals of other groups to speak to. It was all quite stimulating, and I looked forward to the luncheon. These were my expectations of what was inside my box.

With confidence I approached the podium and began with a story about my mom. The audience did laugh at the appropriate time, so I was off to a good start. But then, as I was discussing a technique about removing fears, which asks them to feel uncomfortable stuff, I began to hear talking. I realized that people were starting up their own private conversations. Oh, my God, I thought to myself, I can't believe they're talking while I'm presenting! My confidence was beginning to shake a bit. The energy shifted in the room. Oh, no, I thought, I need to change the energy. I remained on course, spoke my truth, and showed up as me. I didn't sugarcoat the speech. Two people came up to me afterward and said they were going to sign up for my workshop, but as my event contact handed me my payment, I sensed she was uncomfortable.

As I was walking away to begin my uncomfortable exit, another woman approached me from the back of the room. She looked right at me and said, "you are a brave woman." I thought, Okay, brave — hmm, that wasn't exactly what I was expecting. I wonder why I'm brave. She went on to say that when I began speaking about losing my mother to cancer, she had to leave the room because she had lost her daughter a year and a half ago and had been feeling all her tender emotions again lately. She said she was going through a rough time and that she was fine when mingling and walking around but that she couldn't sit still. I asked her if she thought she was avoiding her uncomfortable feelings, running away from her pain and discomfort. She looked right at me and said yes. I told her, "Don't run from them. Face them and feel them so they can leave. Then they won't chase you wherever you go." She thanked me. I never could have helped that woman if I had changed my speech, sugarcoating it to avoid making anyone feel uncomfortable.

But I wanted validation! I wanted the audience to love me and applaud with happiness and have big, warm smiles on their faces. I was disappointed during my ride home. So what was really inside my box? After sitting quietly, I detached myself from the situation and visualized myself as the observer. As the observer, I asked myself, "How did these people benefit?" I realized that many people run away from pain, sensitive issues, fear, or conflict and don't want to look at their inner worlds. My talk urged them to go inside and feel. Most people avoid feeling anything that is troubling them. But feeling is a good thing.

I know I was meant to help that woman who had recently lost her daughter. Luckily, I trusted myself to tell the story about my mom and to follow through with the rest of my presentation regardless of the chatter in the room. The people who were chattering were running, too—they didn't want to feel. People live looking for distracters. When we don't want to deal with things, we shut down, turn off, run and keep busy, play loud music, drink, take drugs, change the subject, use sarcasm, make small talk, live in a state of denial with tunnel vision, live in a fake way, party, travel, and above all, keep moving. We can't force people to learn, grow, take responsibility, and face things, because everyone has his or her own life path, and we must love them just the way they are, without expecting them to be different. Some may never come around and deal with particular life issues, but that's their choice.

We all have expectations, and when our expectations are not what we had imagined, we tend to be disappointed. It's time to take a step back from the situation and ask yourself, what is the real truth in the situation? Try to stay open to what could be inside your box on a deeper level.

Confronting Conflict

Facing conflict can be tough at times, but for our energy to be clean and healthy, it's best to put the cards on the table and get to the real issues in any situation. I believe that many people act in a passive-aggressive way. This can stem from a variety of things. Many people simply are not in touch with their feelings; others keep their feelings inside, guarded; and many are "people pleasers"—they say the things they think the other person would want to hear. For one reason or another, they don't express themselves as situations occur. Therefore, emotions build up and can come out in a very erratic manner. This can happen for several reasons: not having the proper communication skills, not wanting to rock the boat, fear of what the other person will think, fear of rejection or loss, fear of not being "nice," fear of not living in a acceptable way, fear of losing love, or fear that others may discover that one's life is not perfect. People are afraid of dealing with their own uncomfortable feelings, whether loss, rejection, or any other painful emotion. This helps no one. It's imperative not to say anything that you don't mean.

I have learned that things don't need to turn into arguments if we express ourselves properly right when a situation happens. Sometimes we are so shocked by the energy that we don't know how to respond immediately. When that happens, take a deep breath and repeat back what you thought you heard the person say. Then allow the other person to clarify their meaning. It's imperative in life to express how we feel, to take a stand. We mustn't shrink in fear. Confront what life brings you. Conflict just means you are at odds with someone, and dealing with it by communicating can open a door to deeper growth, understanding, compassion, learning, and—who knows?—maybe a stronger relationship, with a newfound respect for each other. I respect people who deal with things by asking questions and not letting things get swept under the rug. Sooner or later, that rug will be so bumpy you'll have to play hopscotch to get over it.

If there is someone in your life you don't like, try this heart-mending visualization:

1. In your visualization, sit comfortably, take a few deep breaths through your nose, and visualize sending this person love. Visualize sending beautiful emerald green light to them and encompassing them with it. Stay with this for a minute, really feeling love inside yourself being sent to this person.

2. Send the intent, respect, and understanding that this person is on their own path. Try to imagine where they are coming from and put your feet in their shoes. Open your mind to a new perspective. Are they looking for appreciation, validation, love, and security? From their perspective, they may have a valid claim or point.

3. See the two of you together laughing, enjoying each other's company with mutual respect.

4. Send them the pure knowing that they are evolving at the most perfect pace for them.

This will alter the energy exchange, and you will be surprised at how quickly it will change. Most people are searching and seeking validation, appreciation, and love. Give people authentically what they need. Like energy against like energy will not defuse a situation. Take the higher road, get out of the ego, and go deeper into your heart for love and compassion.

Our relationships with others will be as deep as we are willing to go within ourselves. If we are not willing to face, deal with, or confront uncomfortable or sensitive issues or feelings, our relationships may be only surface friendships. By facing things, we live a life filled with lessons, healing, energy shifts, increased vibration, and "Ah-ha!" moments, continually seeing things with new eyes. To deepen relationships by creating more intimacy, you must be willing to discuss how you feel by expressing yourself and then being open to any kind of response.

The important thing is to express how you feel. The next step is to do it in a responsible way to get the best results. Don't blame the other person; don't use words such as "you always." This will only put the other person in a defensive mode. Don't say things such as "everyone feels this way," or "Sarah and Joe feel the same way." Keep it between the other person and yourself, and focus on how you feel. And don't analyze the other person; it's not your job to judge them. Don't bring up things from the past that you have already discussed and released. Don't let the other person manipulate or control you by turning the discussion around on you. Stay focused on your issue.

- State the facts only by communicating your feelings.
- Request that the other person repeat back to you what you said.
- Clarify anything that needs to be explained.
- Ask for what you need from the other person by making a reasonable request.
- Listen to them.

Take time daily to write down your thoughts and see if there's anything disturbing you or troubling you that you need to look at. Face your troubles, and they will dissolve away into a stream of inner peace.

Staying Open to Life

Stay open to new possibilities that may occur throughout your day. Staying open to life means you are open to receiving what life has to offer: to meeting and connecting with new people and being open to spontaneity, open to creativity, open to other ways of living and doing things, open to exploring and learning, open to different ways of thinking, open to different ways of making money, open to different ways of believing, open to making last-minute changes. New possibilities will flow into your life when you are open to receiving the unknown. You never know when opportunity will appear. The key is just to be open, accepting, and aware with discernment. Go with the flow and make sure there is a gentle current moving you in your desired direction. If you feel as though you are pushing a boulder uphill, take a look at what you're doing, thinking, and believing. Maybe there's a new direction or a new way to think. Take quiet time to go within and ask for guidance.

Try to stay open to thinking beyond the box to which we can confine ourselves. Don't cling so tightly to how you think everything "should" be in your life. There's a bigger plan than we are privy to; stay more fluid, and go with the current of your life. As you get to know yourself, grow, and expand, you will automatically connect with more life. There's also a bigger message behind everything that happens. What has occurred in your life that you never expected? Where can you see the gift inside your box of family relationships, career, illness, divorce, and death? These gifts are above the misery, struggle, annoyances, disappointment, sadness, hurt, victimization, and pain. They are the gifts of growth; they are the gifts of not taking things for granted, of understanding what is really important, of trusting yourself, of having the courage to handle life, and of an understanding deeper than the current misery you may be in.

Losing a loved one may help you learn to appreciate the other special people you have in your life. Maybe you grew closer to one parent after losing the other, or maybe you and your spouse became closer during the pain of your loss. Some people who have lost a spouse have grown much more bonded with their children. Maybe you will express your true feelings sooner and more easily to others after experiencing loss. Possibly your heart has opened more. Maybe you don't let too much time go by now between visits with the family.

Maybe you don't take life so seriously. Loss is a lesson of appreciation, of not taking people, life, health, or yourself for granted. Appreciate every moment; be present with your family and friends. Don't worry so much about things.

Being fired from a job can be a wonderful gift. It allows you to really look inside the box of minutiae—"Poor me," "Why me?" blah, blah, blah—to see that it could be the divine's way of keeping you on your path, where you're meant to be. I thought at the time it was horrible; I wouldn't let myself relax. I treated looking for a job as a full-time job in itself, faxing résumés all over the country. I was willing to move or even commute to New York from Connecticut. I was sad and felt rejected by the world. I remember crying a lot. I was twenty-nine years old, and I had identified with my job. For me, being without a job meant I was worthless. This came from a place of trying to prove something to my dad; to prove that I was worthy, prove that I could make money. The more money I made, the more I would impress my dad, and the more respect I would get and the more love I would receive.

After being fired from a job in my twenties, my values slowly began to change. I saw how dedicated I had been to my job, checking voice messages multiple times a day while on vacation, keeping my mind firmly fixed on my staff and my job. I felt a lot of stress at night and really lived and breathed my job. After getting fired, I learned what was important—my family and friends—because jobs come and go. I also learned that my career and my job are not my life. They don't own me. I was too busy in my workday for personal calls, and I didn't give my mom or friends my full attention when they called me. I was short with them, and I'm sure it didn't make them feel good. While talking to them, I would be reading e-mails or typing on the computer. Does this sound familiar?

I want my family and friends to know they are the most important people in the world to me. I always have time for the people I care about; after all, you never know how much time you have with anyone. You can strip away everything else—job, home, title, money—family and friends are true wealth. I consider friends extended family; they are people we choose to share our lives with.

When life doesn't go your way, it's a good idea to remember what is really important. Remember all the times you were in a grave situation; perhaps it was a sick loved one, natural disaster, death, or divorce. These situations make you realize what matters. Remember how, when you're going through those times, your everyday struggles go out the window? You're not so concerned about money struggles, pressure from your boss, material things, deadlines, whether your house is perfectly clean or your hair just so. Your focus is now on what you truly care about. When your daily life throws you curveballs, take a breath, hold on, and remember that you are safe; your loved ones are safe. Everything always works out. The light is always there, even when you can't see it.

I believe we do have big things in life to handle, so allow the smaller things to be just that. How we react to these daily curveballs is a test of our character. It's not so much about what is going on; it's how we handle ourselves during the so-called challenges. What are our attitudes and beliefs?

If you are single and in a dating situation, notice how your date handles life when things don't go his or her way. You can learn a lot. Their behavior is a reality check whether this is someone you want to pursue a future relationship with.

Trusting life can be difficult when you feel as though you're living in the unknown. I know it can be scary to trust so much that you don't have to know what your life will look like. This is where faith comes into play. Have faith in the divine and yourself; faith that you will always be okay or even better. This I know is true: if you have trust, life always works out, and even better than you could have imagined.

Appreciate yourself. Do the things you need to do to move forward one day at a time. Be dedicated to attaining your desires, but don't hold on to them too tightly. A friend of mine was going through a tough time with her husband; they were discussing details of their pending separation. She was afraid of what was going to happen. Where were they each going to live? How would they pay the bills? Listening to her, I felt her fear and pain. I looked right at her and told her, "I understand you're upset. I know you can't see it right now, but all this will work out, and you're going to be great. She already is doing great; she's bought a new condo and is in a new relationship. Like I said, one day at a time.

Love without Attachment

True love is being able just to love, without any attachment to getting anything back. This is the purest love: being able to love and open your heart without any expectations. It means loving others just for being who they are, and not trying to change them. Of course, this doesn't imply that they have to become your life partner; you simply love them without expecting anything in return. And this pure love touches others on a deeper level than anything else. This love cradles their spirit and allows their inner light to shine brighter. Wow, what a gift to give someone: true unconditional love! You can express this kind of love to family members, friends, children, your lover, animals, nature, and even people you come in contact with for only a minute in the grocery store. A nod or a warm smile to someone when they most need that human connection and acknowledgment is an expression of pure love.

Love for the pure agenda of only giving. This is done without caring how your love will be received, or what might come back to you from what or whom you love. You may not get it back from that particular person, but it will come back to you in one way or another, from somewhere. When we completely remove all the barriers we create, and open our hearts by getting out of our own way, we are then free to be the divine, perfect beings of light that we truly are.

When we love ourselves we don't have to control others. We trust life so much that we can allow others to be who they are, too, without trying to make them into someone else. After many years of observing married couples throughout my lifetime, I'm convinced that a healthy relationship begins with two healthy people on the roller coaster ride into their own hearts. This relationship will remain healthy if each person respects, loves, and accepts the other exactly as the other is, without the need to control, manipulate, change, or dominate. Respect this person's space, without being their keeper. We are responsible only for ourselves, not for the growth of our partner. No matter how noble our intentions, we do not have the right to mistreat, bully, or control our relationship partners in any way.

Having the courage to do things without being attached to the outcome is often easier said than done. Before doing something, remind yourself of the reason you are doing it. If you're doing it to get a certain response back, then you are attached to that response and you will be upset if you don't receive what you expected. If you are doing something for your own enjoyment, then it won't matter what response you receive.

The good news is, there are many possibilities, many different people for us to have relationships with, an infinitude of different career options, and many homes and cities to live in. The divine is infinitely generous in giving us so many choices in our lives. Don't be attached to the idea that there is only one person for you to marry and spend the rest of your life with until death do you part. This does happen to some people, and it can be beautiful, but if it's not you, know that there are many options for you to meet someone else. If you stay open, trust that you will have other chances for friendships, relationships, careers, and anything else. It's not the end of the world if your favorite dog groomer isn't available anymore. You'll find another one who may be even better. The same applies to your favorite housekeeper, babysitter, accountant, lawyer, stockbroker, plumber, web designer, editor, or publisher. If you are searching for a home and you put a bid on a house and it falls through, that's a sign that you weren't meant to live there. Stay open by trusting that another home will come along in divine timing for you.

Stay detached, trust, be patient, have faith, and your emotions will not be controlled by anyone or anything, because you won't allow it. You won't be "owned" by anyone or anything.

Change

Change is constant; life is fluid; things don't remain the same. Be prepared for movement by detaching yourself from things and staying open to newness—to new things, people, jobs, animals, homes, and life. Make sure your well-being isn't dependent on a situation or person. Situations always change. People change. Our bodies change. Build your foundation with self-love, faith, and inner peace, and you are prepared to withstand anything.

One thing that will always occur in your life is change. How comfortable are you with change? Life happens, and people change jobs, careers, locations, partners, hobbies, focus, desires, and friendships. Most humans are resistant to change. They get comfortable with routine, with knowing their day before it happens. They stay in jobs until they are so miserable it's making them physically or emotionally sick, or they stay in relationships without intimacy for far too long, until one of the partners has an affair or asks for a divorce. This comes out of fear of change, fear of life changing and not knowing what lies ahead. People like what is familiar to them, even though they may not be happy. This is attachment to what they know, what is comfortable to them. It's more comforting to know what to expect, even though it's miserable. It takes faith in the divine to trust in the unknown. Trust in your love for yourself that you don't *need* that job, situation, or person to be happy.

When you stay in an unbalanced relationship too long, it's called dependency on another person. It feels familiar; it's all you've known these many years. You ask yourself, "What will life be like without this person?" You are so afraid because you think you will be alone; you don't think you will find another partner. You don't know how you will support yourself financially or emotionally. You are afraid of hurting or emotionally scaring the children. You are afraid of the children taking sides and wanting to live with your spouse. You are afraid your current friends may side with your spouse. But the divine will support you as long as you support yourself. Take the necessary steps to be in a healthy situation.

By staying in unhappy and unhealthy situations, you are also teaching your children dependency and attachment. Children learn more from how you behave and what you stand for than they will ever learn from your words. Set yourself free! Trust the divine; trust that change is a healthy, positive step for you. We grow bigger in experience through change. Through the continual change of life we learn to detach ourselves from the things we think we need in order to survive — external things. As we age, our looks change and we re-learn how the world responds to us. We have to let go of the idea that we are successful based on how we look. We accept our aging process with grace and know deep down inside that our body is our external representation, which aids us on our particular life journey.

I love this story: A woman was pregnant out of wedlock, and out of fear she told her parents that the father was the Buddha. Her father brought the baby to the Buddha's house and hammered on the door. The Buddha answered, saying, "Can I help you?" Her father handed the baby boy to the Buddha and said, "This is your son." The Buddha said, "So it is," and took the baby into the house. Nine years later, the mother of the baby admitted to her parents that the man working in the fields was the father of her child. Her father went to the Buddha's house and beat on the door. The Buddha and the nine-year-old boy came to the door, and the Buddha said, "Yes, how can we help you?" The father said, "This is not your son; it belongs to the man working in our fields." The Buddha replied, "So it does."

This story represents nonattachment to a person or situation. Now, this is pretty extreme, but what it highlights is the importance of connecting to that deep peace inside you, and the deep connection to faith, spirit, and the divine, knowing that you will always be okay no matter who flows in and out of your life. It is a reminder to tread lightly in life. It also shows a deep understanding of divine order in all life, trusting that everything happens for a reason, that everything happens for growth and learning lessons.

I set an intention at the beginning of every yoga class. In one class, I had noticed some of my yoga students making negative facial expressions or noises while moving from one pose to another. So I decided to set the intention of "embracing transition" at the beginning of the next class. As part of the intention, I urged the students to move from pose to pose with grace, and from there, to change with equal grace in their career, love life, home life, and any other area where they might go through a significant change. We discussed how the ineffectiveness of negative thoughts, struggling, and collapsing in a pose in yoga practice can be applied to life as well. I invited them to see that allowing space for silence, for the gaps of the unknown, is a way of embracing transition. As Wayne Dyer says, "It's really the space between the notes that makes the music you enjoy so much." It's the silence that creates the song.

We spend most of our life in transition, so embrace the transition with ease, comfort, and grace; surrender to a space of faith. After considering these things with the class, I noticed that the students were much smoother in changing poses; I didn't hear any negative comments or grunts, and the energy in the class was much lighter.

When we are projecting an energy of grace, gratitude, and kindness, our bodies will follow suit.

Faith

Faith is the absence of fear. According to Webster's dictionary, faith is "believing without proof." Faith allows you to live a more peaceful life, because you trust that everything always works out. Faith is something you must garner from the depths of your innermost being. It's your foundation for life, and the binding force that carries you through every heartache, every loss, every life transition, every breath. With faith, you feel you are connected to the divine and his helpers—there is no true separation. Our faith is tested from time to time, and at those moments, when we begin to doubt ourselves and our dreams, we are pulling away from faith. We are getting sucked into the energy of "poor me," forgetting who we really are and becoming fearful. Gently bring yourself back to believing in the divine and your own light, by reminding yourself of the truth you really do know: that living in love feels better than living in fear. Faith means that you know:

- You are spirit, an eternal being connected to the divine.
- The divine loves you and forgives you.
- You are here to grow and learn through your life experiences.
- Your unique spirit is needed in the whole divine orchestration of everything.
- You are enough already, just as you are.
- You chose to have this earth experience.
- You believe that everything happens for a divine purpose, in divine timing.
- You are never really alone, because all life is interconnected.
- You believe in yourself and your dreams.

You trust that there will be new opportunities, new people, new relationships, new homes, and new jobs for you. You live open to miracles, and you see the good in everything and everyone. You live in the present moment. You realize that earth is not the only place in the universe. You understand that everything is energy. You surrender to the light within.

When you don't understand why something is happening in your life, ask for extra divine support, for help, love, clarity, and signs. Miracles and magic will happen when you trust and have faith and let go at the same time.

From my experience, it seems a few of my clients who don't have a strong connection to a higher power feel lost and have a hard time trusting life, trusting their own path. I truly believe that if more people believed in the divine or a higher consciousness or universal wisdom or power, and in the universal law of abundance and love, we would live in a happier and more peaceful society. We would have less crime, less violence, less hatred, fewer lawsuits, fewer wars, and fewer natural disasters.

For many years I have been fascinated with the miracles of how life unfolds, how the beautiful pieces of our puzzles come together, how people show up at the right time to share information. I am fascinated with how the divine communicates to us in so many ways: through books, television, license plates, dreams, billboards, magazine articles, songs on the radio, intuition, chills, goose bumps, friends, teachers, family members, strangers, and even by sequences of numbers. We are constantly getting signs from above. I find it inspiring and comforting to know how loved, guided, and supported by spirit we are. I love reading and hearing these types of stories. Pay attention to the many ways signs come into your life. The divine has your back, cheering you on, supporting you with angels by your side, and flooding you with love and inspiration.

Stories that Help Us Increase Our Faith

Six months after I left corporate America, I was working diligently to create my own company. I was also doing some pretty heavy inner work and purging out old behaviors and habits that no longer suited me. I awoke in the middle of the night and looked at the clock; it was 3:33 a.m. The next night when I awoke and looked at the clock, again it was 3:33 a.m. Hmm, I thought, that's pretty interesting, and I wondered if this was some sort of sign. So the next morning I looked up the significance and meaning of those numbers in Doreen Virtue's *Healing with the Angels*. The message in the book stated that the Ascended Masters were with me now. Two days later, a friend called and told me to read a page in another book because she thought I would find the information interesting. (She knew nothing about my experience with the numbers and the message in the book.), After reading her page, I glanced at the facing page, and sure enough, it was a description of what it means to have the Ascended Master guides with you. I felt as if I had been guided through all these "coincidences." Spirit really wanted me to know the significance of what was going on in my life, and why the masters were present at this time. The beautiful beings in spirit are available, and they will find ways to communicate with and support us.

Isn't it wonderful how the divine uses people to support one another in life? Albert Clayton Gaulden has a book that explains this beautifully, called *Signs and Wonders: Understanding the Language of God.* The book defines all the different ways God speaks to all of us and divinely orchestrates things for us. Other books, such as Yitta Halberstam and Judith Leventhal's *Small Miracles* and Neale Donald Walsch's *Moments of Grace,* are full of fun inspirational stories. These books share stories of everyday life in which people are profoundly touched by God.

I had received guidance to write more in this chapter about sign-posts (the various ways the divine gets our attention so we can receive messages), and then I forgot. A couple of days later, while I was visiting with a friend, she said to me, "I'm getting the word 'signposts' for you." She said, "I have no idea what that means, do you?" I said that I was supposed to write more on this topic in my book but had forgotten. This was a situation where spirit used my friend to remind me what I was meant to do.

Within a month of my writing the section in chapter 4, about masculine and feminine energy, my dog trainer was at my house. After leafing through one of the books from my bookshelf, *You Can Heal Your Life*, she told me I should read the paragraph on balancing masculine energy for one of my dogs. And shortly after that, another friend said to me, "I'm hearing that you should write more about masculine and feminine energy."

Neither of these people knew I had already written about that topic in my book. This made me feel that spirit was confirming to me that I was on track with the subject material in my book. We are not alone in this world; spirit is working hard to sprinkle down ideas to us. We just need to pay attention to these signposts. No one is alone in this world. Pay attention; be alert to the signposts; discern and then follow the information.

I was stuck trying to start my car in an outdoor mall parking lot. After many attempts my key would not go into the ignition. I called a friend of mine to come and help me. She tried to put the key in, to no avail. We then prayed for the right person to come along and help us and the very first person to come along was a car mechanic. He had the key in the ignition and the car started within five minutes. Prayer works. Trust in the universe, and the right help will always show up and take care of you.

Raffaella, my very dear friend's mother, was born in Italy, married at a young age to Giuseppe, and moved to America. Raffaella spoke very little English, didn't drive, and relied on her husband for many things. They were best friends. They raised four kids together and were inseparable. Then, in 1985, Giuseppe passed away. This was very hard on Raffaella. She had to create new friends, learn to drive, and live alone for the first time in her life. She was deeply saddened by the loss of her best friend, and husband.

On the fortieth night after Giuseppe died, Raffaella was asleep in her bed, on the same side she had always slept on. Around this time she was very disturbed. She had just found out that the undertaker had put her husband on ice for two days, and the thought of him being cold was agitating to her. Around eleven, she felt her husband lying in his side of the bed, next to her. She felt his arms around her, and he interlaced his fingers with hers. She felt his warm hands and body. She remembers how hot his fingers were. He stayed with her for six or seven minutes, but she was too afraid to turn around and see his face. Once he sensed her fear, he vanished. She knew it was Giuseppe by the way he felt. She felt he had come to reassure her that he was not frozen and cold. She was wonderfully comforted by his visit.

Another night, he visited her again. Raffaella was under some stress about one of her daughters, who was about to give birth to twins. Raffaella was lying in bed when she heard footsteps coming up the stairs. Then the hall light went on, and she got out of bed to see if it was her son. He was sound asleep in his room, though, so Raffaella went back into her room. She then felt her husband, Giuseppe, lying next to her in bed, comforting her. He told her three times, "I feel for you for what you're going through."

Then the hall light went off and she heard the footsteps going back down the stairs. She knew it was her husband, and though she was deeply gratified by his visits, she was scared at the same time. She told him after that not to come anymore, because she was living alone now and it was all just too scary. He has not visited her since.

In September 2003 I flew back east to care for my dad after his neck surgery. What an ordeal that was—one of the toughest weeks of my life besides losing my mom. My dad had checked himself out of the hospital too early and was in great pain over the weekend. I slept outside his bedroom on the couch for two nights so I could help him if he needed anything. Two days later he was in so much pain, we realized his pain medicine wasn't working quickly enough. The doctor had made a mistake writing out the prescription for slow-release instead of quick-release medication, so my poor dad couldn't catch a break from the pain. I was a wreck. I demanded that he go to the hospital with me, and if he didn't listen to me I was going to call an ambulance. I rushed him into the emergency room, and the attending physician gave him more morphine on top of the morphine he already had in his system, and said they would bring him to a room. Feeling terribly upset to see him in so much pain and suffering, I had to leave my dad in the emergency room and drove home to sleep. The next day I went back to the hospital to find my dad really out of it, unable to communicate complete thoughts and not walking or moving very much. The nurse told me she thought something was wrong, and they took him off all medications and were having a CAT scan done on his brain.

I was beside myself, thinking my dad may have had a stroke. He had always been in such consummate control his whole life, and now he had trouble even going to the bathroom. When I called his surgeon in Philadelphia and told him what was happening, the surgeon wanted to helicopter my dad to the hospital where he had had his surgery. His CAT scan and MRI came back showing nothing wrong, so they decided to have him go by ambulance back to the other hospital. I was so emotionally drained and tired at this point, I decided to drive there the next day. Family, friends, and I were all praying for him. By the next day his excruciating pain was all gone; he was walking, talking coherently, and going to the bathroom on his own, even though he had had no pain medication for over twelve hours. I believe that the divine answered these prayers.

Synchronicity

My friend Sue and I have been close for several years now. I have seen and heard her struggles in and out of relationships, trying to find the "right" man with which to marry and settle down. She has been passionate for years about wanting to start a family. With her mother's death a couple of years ago, she had become even more anxious about finding her special life partner. She really put herself "out there," going to bars and parties, dating different men, and even joining an internet dating service. Her world changed forever in one night. Here is her story: Sue was invited to her friend's wedding in July 2003. Her friend decided to play matchmaker. Scarcely able to contain her excitement, she told Sue that she was going to be placed at the same table as a man named Terry. Sue was really looking forward to meeting him, but when she got to the wedding, she realized that Terry had been placed at another table. Needless to say, she was disappointed. At the last minute, the bride's sister had switched the tables and placed him at another table, to meet someone else. Sue ended up saying hello to Terry, but that was the extent of their meeting. In the meantime, Sue remembered a visit she had with a psychic two years before, soon after her mother had died from cancer. The psychic told her that her mother was saying, "The man who gives you pink roses will be the one."

In September, two months after the wedding, Sue went to a beach party, and Terry was there. He asked her to dance, and they were inseparable the rest of the evening, totally taken with each other. A week later, when Terry arrived at Sue's house for a date, he told her he had planned to bring her a bouquet of pink roses from his home. Sue had chills and felt that her mother had sent him to her.

After dating for a couple of weeks, they figured out that this was the second time they were supposed to meet. Sue realized that during the summer, while she was using the internet dating service, Terry was the person she had previously e-mailed responding to his write-up. She had said she was interested in meeting him, but he hadn't responded to her message. Sue and Terry got engaged three months after they met, and they are now happily married and preparing for a family. Terry told Sue that had they met in the summer, it wouldn't have been the right time, because he was still finishing a relationship.

Sue is now a believer in divine timing. When things are meant to happen, life will flow beautifully. Sue's story is a lesson in trusting, praying, believing, and letting it go. We are loved and supported by the many spirit beings that walk with us, and they can take care of the rest. The power of prayer has been both a comfort and a driving force in my life. I hope this story inspires you to have faith in your path and to surrender to the current of life. Know that you don't have to struggle so hard to make things happen. Just put your trusting intention out there to the universe, and have faith that if it's for your highest good, it will happen.

This next story is just one of many that happen to all of us throughout our lives. When we are paying attention to the unfolding of life, we can really appreciate the miracles and all our angelic support.

One day I had the thought that I would like to teach yoga in the senior community. A couple of days later I went to a yoga studio to take my own yoga class. While I was waiting for the class to begin I began chatting with Tim, who was assisting the yoga instructor. He told me he taught yoga at a senior center in town, but that this was his last week because he was moving out of town. I asked him if he needed anyone to take over his class. He said yes and that he would love for me to begin that week. Within four days of our conversation,

I became the Thursday evening yoga instructor at a senior center. I believe it was no coincidences that Tim and I were in the same yoga class at the same time. I believe the universe had a hand in getting us together so we could make a connection. He was looking for a replacement, and I was looking to teach the seniors.

One day I got a postcard in the mail advertising a nearby spa. I thought that this would be a nice getaway, so I told the universe, "If I'm meant to go to this spa, please give me another sign." The next day I was watching television, and a commercial came on for the same spa. I smiled. Deciding that this was a true sign, I picked up the phone and made a reservation for the next night. It was also the right timing to get away for a night. Two hours later I began thinking that I really didn't want to pack up my clothes and deal with the long drive for a one-night getaway. I changed my mind, picked up the telephone, and called the spa back with the intention of canceling my reservation. A woman answered the phone, and I told her I had just made a reservation a couple of hours ago and I would like to cancel. She said, "I'm sorry, no one is here to cancel your reservation. You'll have to call back tomorrow. I told her tomorrow was too late, that I was supposed to be checking in tomorrow. She continued to apologize and tell me no one was there to handle my cancellation. I was shocked and a little angry that I couldn't cancel the reservation that I just made two hours ago.

The next day I drove to the spa, checked into my room, and went down to the store to look at some of their books and other things. While I was sitting down reading a book, a man walked by me. We began talking, and I was curious to get to know him better. I bumped into him the next day and we talked some more. After the trip, we continued communicating and dated all summer long.

It's wonderful how the universe moves us around to meet people, to make connections and relationships. I sometimes wonder if it's challenging or easy for spirit to move us around to be in the precise location at the exact moment. I suppose the more we follow our own intuition, the easier it is for spirit to work its wonders.

"No Worries"

A man sitting next to me on an airplane shared with me his life-altering experience. I was the second person he told his story to.

John and his father were very close—best friends, as he describes it. He and his dad would watch sports together and talk the way best friends talked.

When John was still a teenager, his father died from cancer. Devastated, John became violent and was having a really tough time dealing with life. Three months after his father's death, he was sitting in his den and looked up for some reason. There in the kitchen was his dad, looking at him with a big smile, wearing the sport jacket John had given him years before. John was staring at him in astonishment, unable to fathom what was happening. First he thought it was his imagination, but his father stayed there for over half a minute.

The experience left John feeling a strong sense of love and comfort, and he began to turn his entire life around. Not long after that incident, he was in a severe car accident, hit by a car that ran a light. His seat belt broke, and he was thrown to the other side of the car and crashed through the window. Lying on the ground in shock, John looked up to see his dad on top of his car, giving him the thumbs-up sign.

John walked away from that accident without a scratch on him. His father had saved his life in more ways than one, and at that moment John felt an upwelling of love and appreciation toward the man. His father used to tell him not to worry about anything, that everything always had a way of working out. So after that incident, John told me, he didn't worry about anything anymore. He said there was nothing to worry about.

Visualization

Go to your sacred space. Light incense or candles if you like. Sit in your most natural, comfortable position, with your spine straight, shoulders back, top of your head reaching to the heavens, ears in line with your shoulders. Close your eyes and connect with your breath, breathing through your nose. Bring the breath all the way down to your abdomen; notice how the breath feels coming in and out of your nose. Sit quietly for a minute, just breathing relaxing your whole body and calming the mind. Shift your weight slightly back, to your intuitive side.

Think about the flow of your life. Notice how you felt when you were in the "flow" and things happened serendipitously, doors opened easily, and synchronistic events just happened. Appreciate the beautiful, divine order of these pieces of your life puzzle. Appreciate whom you have become because of those things.

Intention Exercise

I intend to stay open to life.
I intend to confront others when necessary, with compassion.
I intend to live life with faith in God.

Joy Journal

Tell the divine about any conflicts you have in your life. Ask for insight and write down any responses.

Gratitude Journal

Write a list of people who have come into your life with the right information or assistance at a key time. Thank each of them. Hold them in your heart and send them a great big smile of gratitude.

Prayer

Please help me have more faith and trust in the divine.

Please help all beings to see the miracles that are all around them.

Please bring the right people into my life to help me with my projects.

Affirmation

I am able to go with the flow easily, trusting spirit.

I am open to miracles and magic.

I am a peacemaker.

Request

1. If there are people in your life to whom you need to express your feelings in order to clear the energy, do it.

2. Every time a loved one calls you on the phone, let him or her know you have time for him or her. If that moment isn't good, communicate that you appreciate the phone call and want to speak to at a better time. And suggest a time.

3. At the end of each day, write down all the miraculous, synchronistic events that happened to you. Read them aloud. Notice how supported you are!

Chapter 7
Relating with Your Heart

In 1999 I was on a business trip in San Diego. While standing at the registration desk of a conference that I was managing, I decided to call my parents in Connecticut to say hello. My mom was on one phone upstairs, and my dad was on the phone downstairs. My dad announced, "Your mother was just diagnosed with pancreatic and liver cancer. The words crept slowly into my consciousness. What did this mean? At first I didn't grasp the magnitude and severity of the situation.

In shock, I walked back to my hotel room. The next day I flew home to gather my clothes, repack, and fly out the next morning to Connecticut to be with my mom. That evening as I was repacking with a friend of mine, I had tears flooding down my face. My friend had tears pouring down his face as he was listening to me. The life I once knew was changed instantly and forever. I had no idea how much this was going to affect me.

The last five months of mom's life were filled with heartfelt tears, pain, and love for both of us. In a twinkling, all our past squabbles were gone. It all seemed insignificant when I was losing the one person who loved me unconditionally. Feeling as if I was living life in a fog, holding on to an imaginary rope from the divine, I sent daily cries of prayer for my mom to be comfortable and unafraid. In those final months, we shared special moments that opened my heart and healed all past wounds; we were best friends, what I always wanted.

Going through this experience has shown me how strong I can be even when devastated by grief. I didn't run away; I was right by her side for the chemotherapy sessions, watching her arms turn black and blue from all the needles, seeing the disappointment and fright in her eyes, rushing her back and forth to the hospital, dealing with all the emotions, as well as the emotions of friends and family.

I appreciated my ability to love, my inner courage and strength, my ability to be present in the midst of a crisis, my tenderness, and compassion. I released all past hurts between us and just saw her for the woman she was in that moment.

We are not able to escape these intense life moments, but how we choose to be present and how we "show up" is up to us. We all go through loss of loved ones, loss of careers, loss of money, and loss of love. Through these moments come inner strength, courage, compassion, and a deeper love for ourselves.

The ultimate measure of a man
is not where he stands in moments of comfort and convenience,
but where he stands at times of challenge and controversy.
—Martin Luther King Jr.—

Relationships

All relationships are a gift. Our friends and family in life are our teachers. We are learning about ourselves through the relationships. There are times when we will go through up and downs with friends and family, readjustments in the relationships, and even separations, but if we do the best we can, that is all we should expect from ourselves. It's really not that complicated if you just treat each person as you want to be treated. Observe your reactions to situations, notice when you are personalizing something, and go beneath the surface to notice what you are looking for from another person. Notice if there's any communication that needs to be shared.

Through many years of observation, I have been perplexed with how partners and family members treat one another. In most cases, the people we care about the most are the people we hurt the most. Boundaries are crossed, and relationships become burdened with control, manipulation, disrespect, and codependency. I believe we must understand that it's our responsibility to love ourselves first and to know that we are whole and complete. The divine made us whole; we think we are missing something, but we're not.

We must be happy with who we are before we can successfully navigate a romantic relationship; that way we don't rely on someone else to fill that need. We don't want to make another person responsible for our happiness; no one wants that responsibility. Just because two people say, "I do" does not mean we now have the permission and power to tell our partner how to dress, how to drive, when or where to work, how they should spend money, how they should speak, and what they're doing right or wrong. We don't enter a relationship to become a parent or boss; we don't "own" anyone.

A healthy relationship maintains respect and appreciation, with each partner treasuring the other as a gift from the divine and understanding that this person is our best friend, companion, and lover. This person can live life without our directing their every move. Both people have come together to share life, laughter, love, growth, sorrow, change, and newness, through support and compassion. Don't take one minute for granted. Why is it that the people we love the most seem to be the very ones we hurt the deepest? Your partner is also your teacher, teaching you things about yourself, making you more aware of the parts within that you haven't fully accepted or embraced. Think about all the gifts your partner has brought to you.

Family gatherings are always great opportunities to challenge yourself, especially when your parents are making comments you don't agree with, asking the same silly questions, passing on their sage advice to you, or when one of your siblings starts picking on you. You may wonder how you ended up in your family, but keep in mind, it was all divinely orchestrated—with your agreement. The more we accept people exactly as they are, without imposing our own expectations, the more the other person's light can shine. We don't always have to point out to family members what they do wrong. This is part of loving people unconditionally.

Any behavior is just a symptom of the underlying need. When you can respond positively to the emotional need, watch them light up! Notice the occasions when you are around people and they seem to feel good about themselves. Those are times when we love ourselves so much that others feel "bigger"—good about themselves— just by being in our presence. It's important to create a safe space for others in our life to feel vulnerable. When people feel safe and accepted, not judged, they will feel comfortable enough to allow the protective walls that cover their heart to melt away.

This is a gift that allows a deep, intimate connection between souls. To create close, intimate relationships, we must allow ourselves to have our hearts exposed, to allow others to see us for who we really are, to see our hurts, disappointments, and frustrations; but we must be willing to face them ourselves first. If someone isn't ready to go inside and feel what is really there, they will have a hard time creating close, intimate relationships, because they won't allow others to see them for who they really are; they are just not ready to be exposed. They aren't ready to look inside themselves, because it may mean making life changes and feeling pain, and it's too scary.

If you have never been involved in an intimate relationship, maybe that's a sign to begin one with yourself. Trust and believe there is someone out there for you. Get to know yourself first, and then get to know your partner first before getting involved sexually. Allow life to take place and unfold; become friends and learn about each other. Learn whether you like this person—their values, beliefs, temperament, attitude, vision, ethics, compassion, humor, habits, and communication skills, not just how they look. Physical attraction is important, but so is everything else.

I do believe in the sanctity of marriage, and that married couples can be healthy and happy. I also believe that if people choose to be together without getting married, that is what is meant for them, and it, too, is perfect. There are plenty of sources out there for getting help in the art of communication and relationships through therapy, marriage counseling, books, CDs, and workshops.

If your family is your priority, then energy will go in that direction. Many people suffer through the same fights, using the same fighting techniques without resolving anything for years, and it's quite sad to see. They just don't know any better. They get frustrated and nothing changes, and they don't take the time to learn communication techniques. Dr. Marshall Rosenberg is one of many people with good videos, books, and workshops on the art of nonviolent communication. Here's my formula for relationships:

- Invite the divine into your heart and bless your relationships.
- Respect each person's beliefs, feelings, personal space, interests, and desires.
- Say "please" and "thank you."
- Forgive and let go.
- Allow yourself to be vulnerable.
- Say you're sorry.
- Take responsibility for your thoughts, words, and actions.

- Don't make assumptions—ask for clarification.
- Be trustworthy and honest.
- Ask for what you want without attachment to the outcome.
- Speak in a civil manner and tone of voice, without resorting to name-calling, cursing, or derogatory remarks.
- Show appreciation and gratitude.
- Be a good listener without interrupting.
- Be true to your own heart and be yourself.
- Show sincere interest.

Love and learn from one another. Enjoy and appreciate the time you spend together. Encourage each other to be yourselves, and follow your dreams together. Appreciate your partner; allow their inner light to shine. Accept your partner for who they are, without needing to make them into someone else. You are two individuals sharing life together. You both have your own individual desires, needs, and life lessons. Bless each other and stay connected through touch, communication, listening, and spending time together.

We have a different relationship with each person in our life. Some relationships are more intimate than others; we must be ready to look at our own behavior and grow with the relationship and not pull away from it. Some relationships are meant to end, while others can survive the truth, depending on whether the connection is healthy for both people. We have choices. We can choose not to look at our stuff, blame the other person for a thousand different reasons, make them wrong, create drama, and hold on to our righteous hurt and stay stuck, or we can think over and pray over our issues, see what we can learn from them, and grow through it.

Instead of telling someone what *you* think they should do, and without falling into the energy of judging, hold the space of seeing them as whole. You can do this for your kids, friends, partner, spouse, coworkers, subordinates, and even yourself. See the person as already capable. See them as secure, confident, loving, happy, powerful, healthy, and successful, and hold the absolute knowing that they will succeed—that they already are successful. See them through eyes of beauty and nonjudgment, through the eyes of the divine. Let them know that you love them no matter what they decide or how they respond or act. This is showing respect for their spirit. You are just guiding them back to their own divine remembrance of who they truly are.

My coaching practice has taught me that one of the best ways to empower someone is to let them make their own decisions. One way to do this is by asking very pointed, powerful questions. These questions help people to clarify, discover things from a higher or different perspective, removing limiting beliefs and staying empowered at the same time. Such questioning and reflection allows people to deepen their awareness by holding a sacred space for them, honoring their own path and divinity. I act as a catalyst for their own self-discovery merely by guiding them back to what is already there inside them—to their own internal teacher. I hear often "I do know this but I just forgot"; "That just clicked, and I'm having an 'Ah-ha!' moment"; "The lightbulb just went off"; and "That is a different way of looking at it, but I understand." This is very important. It allows people to keep their power and come to their own conclusions, which enables them to build trust within themselves. And that is the most important thing.

Visualization

Invite the highest vibration of love and truth to surround you— call on the divine, your spirit guides, angels, and your higher self. Go to your sacred space in or outside your home. Light incense or candles if you wish. Sit comfortably, with your spine straight, shoulders back, top of your head reaching to the heavens, ears in line with your shoulders. Close your eyes, and begin to connect with your breath, breathing through your nose. Bring the breath all the way down to your abdomen; notice how the breath feels coming in and out of your nose. Sit quietly for a minute, breathing in and out, calming the mind. Shift your weight slightly back, toward your intuitive side.

Imagine white light coming in from the divine with each breath, and allow it to penetrate your whole being. Connect your light to the white light from the divine. Visualize any situation in your life that you would like to see through eyes of joy. Ask the divine to help you see and feel this joy while you are in this situation in your life. Visualize the angels supporting you. Feel their comfort and unconditional love surrounding you. Know that you are supported even in this time or this situation in your life. Visualize a long rope from the divine coming down from the heavens. You are holding on to this rope. This is your life support and your connection. Feel the inner peace coming from your own soul. The place that knows that nothing can hurt the pure love and light of who you are—the place of pure wisdom. Release your pains and troubles to the divine, and surrender into your own peace. Breathe in peace throughout your whole body.

Intention Exercise

I intend to surrender all unnecessary pain to God, to turn into love and light. I intend to spend more time with my family. I intend to be at peace around my family.

Prayer

Please bless all my relationships.

Please help me open my heart and allow my perfect relationship to enter my life.

I pray that my loved one in spirit is happy and safe, and I send her/him love.

Joy Journal

Write your own story about how you were able to find the joyous moments in the midst of a very difficult period in your life.

Gratitude Journal

What have you learned from your mom? Make a list of all the positive traits and teachings you have received from your mom. What lessons have taught you to have more compassion in your life? Make a list of five positive qualities of each family member. Focus on those qualities that you appreciate, and share them with each person.

Affirmation

I am a loving friend.

I am a wonderful lover and spouse.

I am a compassionate and loving daughter/son.

Request

Reflect on the love you have in your life, especially with your family and friends. Make a list of five ways you can show each of them how much they matter in your life. Each day choose a person from your list and express your appreciation. Let them know how important they are to you.

Conclusion

Blessings to you on your life journey into your heart! This book is meant to be interactive. It's as if you were getting your own personal coaching sessions, complete with homework and much to ponder. For a deeply penetrating, transformational effect right down to the cellular level, use the book as a complete coaching guide, answering the thought-provoking questions, following through on the exercises, and practicing the suggestions.

It's meant for you to have an experience of what I'm talking about, by doing the visualizations and exercises at the end of each chapter as well as using the tools and exercises that appear within the chapters. To change behavior and beliefs or create new patterns and habits; you will benefit the most by doing it, living it, and feeling it. Reading the book is not enough. Play with the visualizations and allow yourself to be creative and maybe come up with your own way of doing something.

With deep respect, God bless you.

About the Author

Laurie Martin is a champion for self-love, truth, and conscious-ness. After fifteen years of corporate business experience, she re-signed as Vice President of Worldwide Events for a publicly-traded company and is now a certified Life Coach. Through her tenacious perseverance during a spiritual awakening, she found herself on the other side of fear. Since then she's led hundreds of people out of the web of fear into a world of new knowledge and wisdom. Lau-rie has spent many years giving uplifting, inspiring, and empower-ing workshops, coaching clients, teaching hatha yoga, and writing. Her inspirational articles have been published online in Evan Carmi-chael's website, Motivation and Strategies for Entrepreneurs, which has 150,000 monthly hits. Her own newsletter has been distributed monthly for over five years around the world. She is also a member of Naples Woman's Group, an organization that improves the status of women worldwide. She can be reached at her website:
www.SmileAcrossYourHeart.com

Books from Yes International Publishers

Justin O'Brien, Ph.D.
    Walking with a Himalayan Master: An American's Odyssey
    Superconscious Meditation
    A Meeting of Mystic Paths: Christianity and Yoga
    The Wellness Tree: Dynamic Program Creating Optimal Wellness
    Running and Breathing
    Mirrors for Men: A Journal for Reflection

Linda Johnsen
    A Thousand Suns: Designing Your Future with Vedic Astrology
    The Living Goddess: Tradition of Mother of the Universe
    Daughters of the Goddess: Women Saints of India
    Kirtan! Chanting as a Spiritual Path (with Maggie Jacobus)

Theresa King
    The Spiral Path: Explorations in Women's Spirituality
    The Divine Mosaic: Women's Images of the Sacred Other

Phil Nuernberger, Ph.D.
    Strong and Fearless: The Quest for Personal Power
    The Warrior Sage: Life as Spirit

Swami Veda Bharati
    Subtler than the Subtle: The Upanishad of the White Horse
    The Light of Ten Thousand Suns

Prem Prakash
    Three Paths of Devotion

Ron Valle and Mary Mohs
    Opening to Dying and Grieving: A Sacred Journey

Rev. Alla Renee Bozarth
    Soulfire: Love Poems in Black and Gold

Charles Bates
    Pigs Eat Wolves: Going into Partnership with Your Dark Side

Mary Pinney Erickson and Betty Kling
    Streams from the Sacred River: Women's Spiritual Wisdom

Cheryl Wall
    Mirrors for Women: A Journal of Reflection

Gopala Krishna
    The Yogi: Portraits of Swami Vishnu-devananda

Christin Lore Weber
    Circle of Mysteries: The Women's Rosary Book

Laurie Martin
    Smile Across Your Heart: The Process of Building Self-Love